MW00440554

Dharma Drum

Dharma Drum:

The life and heart of Ch'an practice

Ch'an Master Sheng-yen

Dharma Drum Publications

90-56 Corona Avenue, Elmhurst, New York 11373

Managing Editor: Ven. Guo-gu Bhikshu
Editors:Sebastian Bonner, Alicia Minsky
Editorial Assistants: Lisa Commager, Harry Miller, Linda Peer
Translators: Chia-hui Lin, Ven. Guo-gu Bhikshu
Cover calligraphy:Xi Zeng
Interior calligraphy: P. L. Jin, Xi Zeng
Photos: Bernard Handzel, Linda Peer
Interior design and Typography: Trish Ing
Cover design: Stephen Morse

The first four chapters in Part One are revised versions of talks previously published in the *Ch'an Newsletter*. The last two chapters in Part One are selected and revised from *Zen Wisdom: Knowing and Doing*.

FIRST EDITION

Library of Congress Catalog Card Number 95-83637
ISBN 0-9609854-8-4

法 鼓

著者／聖嚴法師　　出版者／紐約法鼓出版社
台灣發行所／法鼓文化事業股份有限公司
總經理／張元隆
地址／台北市北投區大業路 260 號 6 樓
Tel/(02)2893-4646　Fax/(02)2896-0731
在台初版／1998 年 6 月
建議售價／新台幣 500 元
郵撥帳號／1877236-6　　戶名／法鼓文化
登記證／行政院新聞局局版北市業字第 176 號

Contents

Introduction

 F or those who are interested in following the Path of Ch'an (Zen), *Dharma Drum* will guide and inspire both study and practice. By teaching us how to bring the practice of Ch'an into everyday life, Master Sheng-yen offers a fresh understanding of the connections linking body and mind, as well as glimpses into the meaning and purpose of our interactions with others.

The compassion and wisdom that make this book a guiding voice are the expressions of an enlightened man, one who beats the Dharma Drum to benefit all people. Master Sheng-yen is one of the foremost living masters in the Buddhist tradition, receiver of transmissions from both the Ts'ao Tung (Jp. Soto) and Lin-chi (Jp. Rinzai) traditions of Ch'an. Born on a farm outside Shanghai in 1930, Sheng-yen became a monk at the age of thirteen. In 1949, during the Communist takeover, he moved to Taiwan to continue his study and practice. One night, nearly ten years later, he found himself speaking at great length to Ch'an Master Ling-yuan about the difficulties and doubts he struggled with in his practice. Suddenly, Master Ling-yuan said, "Put down!" At that moment Master Sheng-yen shattered all doubts, let go of all his attachments and experienced his initial enlightenment.

In 1963 Master Sheng-yen began a six-year solitary retreat in the mountains. After the retreat, Master Sheng-yen earned his master's degree and doctorate in Buddhist literature from Rissho University in Japan, and then devoted himself to stemming the decline in Chinese Buddhism by reviving the tradition of rigorous education for monks and nuns.

Over the years, his activities in this arena have created a widespread, increasingly international dissemination of the study and practice of Buddhism. Since 1978, he has served as abbot of Nung Ch'an Monastary in Taiwan, where over sixty nuns and monks currently live and practice. In 1985, he founded the Chung-Hwa Institute of Buddhist Studies, a graduate school based in Taiwan. And 1998 will see the opening of Dharma Drum Mountain, an international monastary and Buddhist university located near Taipai. Master Sheng-yen has also worked tirelessly to spread the Buddhadharma in this country. Since 1978, when he first came here at the invitation of the Buddhist Association of the United States, he has established the Ch'an Meditation Center, located in Queens, New York, and lectured and taught widely throughout the United States.

A word now about this book's title: the Dharma Drum is often mentioned in Mahayana Buddhist scriptures such as the *Great Dharma Drum Scripture* (*Maha-beri-haraka-parivarta-sutra*) and the *Lotus Scripture* (*Saddharma-pundharika-sutra*). The thundering sound of the Dharma Drum symbolizes the teaching of the Buddha, the teaching that awakens living beings from their long dream of "birth and death." *Dharma Drum* signifies the teaching beyond all words and language that points to the realization of our Mind and meaning of our existence. All Ch'an teachings are the thundering sound of the Dharma Drum, in that they release us from vexations and conditioning, nurture our innate wisdom and compassion to the highest extent, and reveal our hidden potential. When we listen to the Drum, we discover the path to Buddhahood.

As mentioned above, Dharma Drum Mountain will soon become an international monastic and educational complex under the direction of Master Sheng-yen. The activities planned for Dharma Drum Mountain can be grouped into two categories. The first category includes scholarly research in Buddhism and the promotion of Buddhist teachings: Dharma Drum Mountain will publish both scholarly and Buddhist works, as well as offer instruction to students at high school, university, and graduate levels. The second category will encompass cultivation activities. Long and short term Ch'an meditation retreats and Buddha's Name recitation retreats will be held regularly, and will accommodate people of all ages and levels of practice. Solitary Ch'an retreats are also available for those who have practiced for a long time and gained a deep understanding of Ch'an. Master Sheng-yen's vision, cultivated over many years of practice and realized in the creation of Dharma Drum Mountain, is to uplift the character of mankind and shape this world into a pure land. For this reason, we named this book *Dharma Drum*, dedicating it to the project in Taiwan.

Though the book began as a straight translation of another Chinese book written by Master Sheng-yen, I soon found that some of the ideas originally written for a Chinese audience would, because of cultural differences, be irrelevant to a Western reader. While keeping half of the original manuscript, I gathered new materials already published in our Ch'an Magazine and Newsletter and retranslated articles from Chinese that spoke to the needs of a Western audience.

The book, is therefore, divided into two parts. Part one is pedagogical in nature, in that its discussions of practice deal with practical, directive explanations of conceptual and historical developments within Ch'an and Buddhism. Part Two pulls the reader into the lyrical rhythms of Ch'an practice; the aphorisms and anecdotes are distillations of Dharma talks given by Master Sheng-yen which have been published in both Chinese and English. Each paragraph in Part Two stands on its own, waiting for the reader's understanding; each paragraph should be practiced. Some of Master Sheng-yen's comments may seem abstract, but as one's practice deepens, they reveal their profundity and helpfulness. Overall the book can be appreciated by people at any level of practice. Beginners may find the glossary especially helpful in understanding the different ideas and levels of Buddhist terminology.

This book was initiated in Taiwan by Mrs. Chia-hui Lin, a student of Master Sheng-yen, whom I am very grateful. Very special thanks to her father Mr. Chin-shiang Lin for generously funding this entire project through the

Lin Pan Cultural and Educational Foundation.

I thank Dale Crowley, a student of Master Sheng-yen who now resides in Hong Kong, for proofreading and urging me to retranslate this book in 1994. He and I spent a fair amount of time together working on this book after an intensive Ch'an retreat when we were both in Taiwan. Sebastian Bonner, a friend of our center in New York who had previously helped in editing a book by Master Sheng-yen, was kind enough to edit, read and suggest changes for this book. Very special thanks to Alicia Minsky, a professional editor based in New York, who edited and polished the final manuscript with Sebastian.

Although we sometimes encounter difficulties when we use English to convey Buddhist ideas and language in Master Sheng-yen's talks, we have tried to retain his vitality, humor, and directness. I am grateful to all of the people above mentioned and many others who helped in making this project possible. May the sound of *Dharma Drum* be heard throughout the world.

Ven. Guo-gu Bhikshu
Ch'an Meditation Center
New York , 1995

Part One

Dreaming
Asleep
and
Awake

T he Buddha described the consciousness of waking life as a dream. Acceptance of life as a dream may be difficult, especially if life seems to offer contentment and happiness. No one likes to be awakened from a pleasant dream, let alone be told that his life amounts to nothing more than illusions.

But how can we distinguish between dreaming and waking? According to the Buddha, sleep is made up of short dreams, but life is a long dream. You may awaken to the fact that you are living a dream, and then fall back into the dream once again. In Buddhism, awakening from the long dream of life means realizing your self-nature. A sentient being who does not experience this realization remains forever caught in a dream.

Everything is fleeting, everything is unreal. We think of our dreams as unreal and believe our waking moments to be reality. But when we recognize the illusory nature of the body, of the world, of life and death, we then see that both sleeping and waking are equally dreamlike states.

A famous Chinese photographer, Lang Jing-shan, takes pictures of the areas around the Yellow and Yangtze Rivers, and makes them resemble Chinese "mountain and water" paintings. The whole image becomes an impression built from fragments. This is how our minds work. Our experiences are stored as fragments in the subconscious mind. We never remember experiences in their entirety, but rather in bits and pieces. At a certain time or place, the fragments may reappear in our consciousness. And so it goes when we dream.

Perhaps you experience *déjà vu* when you see or read something that you believe you've already seen or read. We all have many experiences and thoughts that trigger feelings and responses in our minds. But like impressionistic photographs, these responses are merely fragmentary, illusory reflections of our experiences, thoughts, and fantasies.

Few people know when they are dreaming; fewer still want to wake up once they discover they are dreaming. Someone who does not see his self-nature thinks he is very much awake, that life is real, and that he does not suffer. When he recognizes the illusory nature of the self, he realizes that he has only been dreaming a very long dream and that this dream is indeed marked by suffering. But relatively few people appreciate that recognizing the impermanent and illusory nature of everyday life requires serious daily practice. It is not enough to merely listen to my words, read a book or reach an intellectual understanding of the concept. Many have heard about Buddhist practice, but few want to really commit to it. Rarer still is the person who practices, awakens from the dream, and, rather than falling back into the dream, comes to realize his self-nature.

A well-known Chinese folktale, "Dream of the Millet," tells the story of a young man who traveled to a capital city to take the civil examination that would qualify him as a government official. On the road he met an old man who was cooking millet. The old man saw that the young traveler was tired, gave him a pillow, and told him to rest. The young man lay down and fell into a long dream.

He dreamed that he achieved the highest score in the examination. Then he married a princess and became the prime minister at the imperial court. He kept many concubines and by the time he reached his hundredth year, his children were too numerous to count. He enjoyed his long life and even in old age he did not want to die. But when the time came for him to die he could not avoid it and, as everyone must, he passed away. After he died, two demons led him down to the underworld because he had abused his bureaucratic power and embezzled court funds. He was punished by the judge of the dead and made to climb a mountain of knives, after which he was thrown into a vat of boiling oil. He felt a tremendous pain and screamed. Just then the old man woke him up and told him that the millet was ready.

It had only taken two hours to prepare the millet, but in the dream the young man experienced the passing of a hundred years. Time passing quickly is a common experience, not only in dreams, but in daily life. Sometimes we have dreams that seem very long but which really last only a few minutes of waking time. Differing perceptions of time also occur when we do sitting meditation. If your legs hurt and you can't concentrate, the time seems to crawl, but if your legs feel fine and concentration is not a problem, the time flies.

Dreams are by nature illusory and passing, and our consciousness of time and reality also passes like a dream. But it is a mistake to think that our actions in waking life are as inconsequential as those in dreams. We may not have to suffer the consequences of our actions in dreams, but we cannot avoid those consequences in waking life. Our actions and speech create strong and lasting effects that do not fade away as easily as dreams do. This is the principle of cause and consequence.

Most people think that they are not responsible for their thoughts if they do not act on them. All of us have bad thoughts we never act on: wanting to have everything we see, wanting to harm someone we don't like, and so forth. Even the most devoted mothers sometimes think about killing their own children when they cry too loudly. For the most part, we do not believe these thoughts break the Buddhist precepts against lying, killing, misconduct, and stealing. But for a bodhisattva, harboring such thoughts is tantamount to breaking the precepts. Few people think about striking or killing someone when they sit in meditation. But in their sleeping dreams and the course of daily life, violent and murderous thoughts may arise quite often. Anyone who practices regularly, who adopts the attitude of a bodhisattva, needs to let go of such ideas both in sleep and in daily living.

While dreaming, people often experience nonvirtuous

thoughts or perform nonvirtuous actions. That is because such thoughts reside in their minds. But truly advanced practitioners do not dream of wrongdoing, just as they do not break the precepts while awake. This equivalence is called correspondence of thought and action. Noncorrespondence, on the other hand, implies that a person does not break the precepts while awake, but still has wrongful thoughts when dreaming. An anecdote from my teaching experience offers a useful analogy of noncorrespondence: Several years ago, an electrical blackout plunged one of my classes into darkness. The students all began to shout and laugh. Why? Their hidden minds emerged. They exhibited self-control in the light, but felt free in the darkness.

Although we may understand that our lives are vain, unreal and dreamlike, we still bear responsibility for this sleeping and waking dream. Just as the activity of the body creates karma, so does the activity of the mind. For example, if you do not know someone is behind you, you might accidentally step on his foot and then apologize. In such a case you would not feel as though you had done anything particularly wrong. Likewise, according to a bodhisattva's perspective, the acts of the body are not serious, but those of the mind are. For ordinary sentient beings, however, the karma of the body is more serious than that of the mind.

Because the bodhisattva way is based on mental realization, we should understand that karma caused by the body means little compared to karma created by the mind. So, we should pay attention to our mental behavior and take responsibility for it. We must make our minds simple, peaceful and tranquil. Sincere and rigorous practice lets us calm both body and mind, which in turn allows us, day by day, to reduce our karmic obstructions.

Transforming
Suffering

From the moment we enter the world, the threat of illness hovers over us. The person who has not suffered illness has yet to be born, and only after death does illness cease. And suffering is not limited to the body; the lives of sentient beings are marked by mental as well as by physical suffering. Indeed, a physically healthy person with a sick mind suffers far more than a person whose body is ailing, but whose mind is strong and healthy.

Buddhism began in India about 2500 years ago when Sakyamuni Buddha addressed the problem of suffering. The Buddha saw that it was more important to help the mind than the body; he advised seeking medical help to relieve physical ailments, but following and practicing the Buddhadharma to alleviate mental suffering.

Physical illness involves pain, which is nothing more than a bodily sensation; mental illness involves suffering, which distorts sensation, magnifies our problems, and makes our lives miserable. Buddhadharma does not rid us of bodily pain. It is not an anesthetic. Buddhadharma helps us to alleviate and then rid ourselves of mental suffering. When all mental problems are cured, that is liberation.

According to Buddhism, there are three causes of suffering:

1. Beginningless ignorance. Western religions talk about a beginning; western science theorizes about the origins of the earth and the universe. But where is the starting point of a circle? Try as you might, you cannot find it. And when did suffering originate? Buddhism says that there is no beginning, that sentient beings have experienced suffering since beginningless time.

2. The cause and consequence cycle of vexations. The consequences we experience now stem from previous causes. In turn, these present consequences become the causes for future consequences. As we move forward in time, we never cease to create further causes.

3. Vexations. The vexations from which we suffer arise from our environment, our relationships, and from emotional turmoil.

The Environment

On a recent lecture tour, I had the opportunity to visit the city of San Francisco. The climate there is quite varied: fog and wind interrupt calm, clear skies, and the temperature can change in a heartbeat. It came as no surprise to me that while some people consider San Francisco a heaven on earth, others find it a place of suffering. During my visit, I rode in a car with a woman who kept sneezing. I asked her, "Are you sick?" She said, "No, I'm just allergic to the air." Imagine! Even in San Francisco, people suffer from the climate, from pollutants and diseases carried by the air, even from microbes found in food. Indeed, any environment can be a great cause of vexation.

Relationships

Relationships often cause a great deal of suffering. But who is responsible for most of our vexations? Most people think that their enemies is the source of misery. This is usually not the case. More often, the culprit is one of our family members, perhaps a close friend, or, not least, a professional colleague. To give you an example of the latter case: recently, after giving a lecture at Stanford University, I found myself surrounded by scholars, who spent the evening complaining the fact that scholars were such petty people.

Ideally, of course, we should help and support each other. The last thing we should do is tear each other down. But the fact is that people hinder more often than they help each other. And intelligence is no safeguard against the basic pettiness and competitiveness that riddles human nature. Is there anyone who has never set himself against another? The answer is no.

Emotional Turmoil

We are vexed most by the enemy within – our own minds. Our thoughts, feelings, attitudes and perceptions change constantly. We can move from arrogance to regret, from joy to sorrow, from hate to love, in a matter of seconds. As time passes, our point of view changes, so that we look at something old in an entirely new way. But when we are caught in a turmoil of thought and feeling, we feel conflicted and powerless to make decisions. We worry about gain or loss, right or wrong. So much indecision throws us into a tumultuous, vexed state of mind. And though everyone suffers in this way, many people insist that they have no problems. Some even throw tantrums and work themselves into frenzies in their attempts to prove to you that their troubles have nothing to do with them.

I once asked someone directly why he had so many vexations. "It's not me!" he cried, "it's the other rotten people who are making me so miserable." In fact, most of his problems were self-created.

Recently, I was riding in a car with four people who were involved in a heated discussion. One said to me, "Sorry that we argue so much, Shih-fu." I replied," You're the ones arguing; it's none of my business." I heard what they said, but chose not to take part in or be affected by their conversation. The following morning, one of the four said, "I cannot stand to hear people argue. The very sound of it upsets me." Do you understand? His vexation stems from his own intolerance.

According to Buddhism, mental vexation can come in the form of greed, anger, ignorance, arrogance, or doubt. Whenever you are distressed, analyze the nature of your vexation. As soon as you determine which category your vexation falls into and reflect on it, the intensity of your vexation will diminish. When you are distressed by greed, for instance, you can collect yourself by reflecting, "Ah, there's greed arising again; I do have strong desires!" Be

objective and non-judgmental, and the vexation of greed
will automatically diminish. Similarly, when you suffer from
anger: "Why am I so angry? My distress is directly related
to my anger." In this way both the distress and the anger
will subside. Look inward. You don't need to analyze the
problem; you need to examine your own mind. When you
have done something foolish and feel miserable about it,
let yourself see the action for what it is, and then reflect, "I
have acted foolishly." Simply accepting your weakness in a
particular situation will lighten your vexation and suffering.
You should reflect in the same way on suffering caused by
arrogance. Simply being aware of arrogance will help you
overcome feelings of pride and self-righteousness.

Doubt can also create suffering. Doubt will prevent you
from making decisions, in that it obstructs your ability to
trust yourself and others. If you know that you suffer from
doubt, reason as follows: "I want to accomplish a task, so
I'd better believe that I have the ability to do so and that it
is the right thing to do." If you allow yourself to trust this
reasoning, you will most likely accomplish whatever you
wish to do.

The invidious influence of doubt can taint and mar our
lives. Imagine a man who has decided to marry, but who is
plagued by doubt. He wonders if the marriage will end in
divorce, or if his future bride will leave him, or if she has
lied or withheld something important from him. If he does
not check his doubt, he will be miserable at the prospect of
marriage and miserable within the marriage. Indeed, even
if a couple has no real cause to break up, doubt can furnish

the reason and cause marital problems. If you have such doubts, say to yourself: "If I really have so many doubts, then it's foolish for me to marry. If I want to marry, I need to accept and trust my partner." If you cannot let go of at least some of your doubt, then perhaps you would be better off remaining single.

Is there anyone who has no doubts whatsoever? I have yet to meet that person.

Buddhism describes five general causes of mental disturbance:

1. Pursuing objectives without considering your strengths and weaknesses. Perhaps you are not aware of the resources you possess and so are never satisfied with your efforts. Or when faced with a situation that is beyond your control, you torment yourself with the desire to fight against inevitable circumstances. For instance, many people, especially young people, believe their potential is unlimited. What they see others have accomplished, they believe they too can achieve. When adverse conditions arise, however, they feel personally wronged and resist, rather than understand, their situation.

2. An insatiable desire to expand and conquer. People who suffer from this disturbance always needs to magnify their abilities, successes, or possessions. Such people want to extend their influence beyond all limits. Some strive for fame so that the world will see their name in lights. Others use power directly to conquer those who oppose them. Such power struggles can occur between nations, within families or relationships: one nation wants to take over another; a

wife wants to conquer a husband, or *vice versa*. Such desire to overcome others, be it global or conjugal, is a mental disturbance.

3.   Arrogance over achieving a particular objective or station. Pride and self-satisfaction can lead to callousness and a general disregard for others. An arrogant person believes that he or she has the right to hurt others or sweep them aside according to personal whim.

4.   Despair over failing to achieve a goal. When you get very discouraged, lose confidence in yourself, and blame others for your failures, you give rise to despair.

5.   Insecurity due to doubt. Confidence evaporates when the mind bubbles with uncertainty.

I am neither a psychiatrist nor a psychologist. I am not versed in the standard classifications of mental illness. I know only the Buddhist point of view, which divides mental problems into the five categories described above. These five disturbances in turn can generate a myriad of other mental problems. Note, however, that Buddhism is not concerned with the causality or pathology of the particular elements that lead to a person's mental distress. Buddhism deals only with the recognition and elimination of mental disturbances.

Now, how can we balance the mind and treat its ailments?

People often confront their mental disturbances with ineffective methods. They either deny their vexations, insisting, "I am not sick. I have no problems. There is nothing wrong with me!" Or they attempt to treat themselves via a continual mental review of their faults and a continuous round of misguided remedies. Such methods build one false assumption on another, and end up making matters worse for the sufferer.

Psychiatrists and psychologists use insight-based talk therapies to analyze and explain their patients' problems. Although the aim of such therapies is to help the patient come to his or her own realization, Buddhadharma views such methods as temporary and incomplete. The doctor can discover only part of the problem, so the patient never sees the complete picture of his illness. Problems often recur even after extensive counseling. Sometimes patients languish in therapy for ten or twenty years. This should be enough to make the doctor sick.

The Buddhist method of healing can be divided into two broad categories: change of concepts and methods of practice.

Change of Concepts

1. The concept of cause and consequence

Buddhists have faith that there was a life before this life, and one before that, and so on through innumerable past lives. Much of what we experience now may seem unfair, but it is simply a consequence of actions we have performed in the past. Our willingness to accept what befalls us, good or bad, depends on our willingness to accept the concept of cause and consequence. This concept extends beyond religious belief into a well-known fact of everyday life. No matter what we do, our actions have consequences.

2.   The concept of causes and conditions

All phenomena arise and pass away because of the accumulation and interaction of different conditions. The cause of a flower is a seed, but soil, water, and sun must be present for the plant to come into existence. Time, uprooting, or lack of water or sun will cause the plant to wither and die.

Ch'an stresses the importance of having faith in the Dharma, or teachings of the Buddha. These teachings assure us that everyone has Buddha-nature and that everyone can attain Buddhahood. Every human being who truly has faith in the teachings of the Buddha, who follows Buddhist principles and methods of practice, can become a Buddha.

People usually wish others to be compassionate towards them, but seldom remember that they should exercise compassion towards others. There are those who, when they make a mistake, demand that they be forgiven. "Don't measure me against the standards of a saint!" they cry. But if they see someone else err, they're quick to say, "You're incompetent. Why couldn't you do it right the first time?"

You can develop and nurture a spirit of compassion by actively observing four criteria:

–   Understand your own conflicts and cultivate inner harmony.
–   Feel sympathy for other people's shortcomings.
–   Forgive other people's mistakes.
–   Concern yourself with other people's suffering.

The first criterion is especially important. In order to be at peace with yourself, you must develop and maintain a calm and peaceful mind. You can cultivate such inner calm and peace by keeping in mind the concepts of cause and consequence, cause and conditions. If you maintain an awareness that your actions have consequences, and that trying situations arise out of conditions created by your own karma, you will experience compassion, sympathy, forgiveness, and caring towards others.

Methods of Practice

1.   Mindfulness of the Buddha, which involves reciting the Buddha's name. There are two reasons for this practice. First, reciting the Buddha's name in order to be reborn in the Pure Land gives you hope for the future and, consequently, makes it easier for you to let go of the present. Second, reciting the Buddha's name can alleviate your mental problems. When you find yourself psychologically off-balance, you can remove anger, doubt, or other mental disturbances by concentrating on the Buddha's name. I often tell people, "Whenever you want to yell at someone, recite Amitabha's name." You will be sending your anger to Amitabha. Let it be the Buddha's problem!

2.   Meditation

Sitting meditation can collect a scattered mind and stabilize mental disturbance. There are many methods of meditation and many levels of attainment, all of which will be explained in the following chapters. At this point, let me simply give you an idea of the more profound stages you might experience from meditation, namely, the stages of samadhi and no-mind.

When you achieve the state of samadhi, you reach the point where no wandering thoughts exist in your mind. In samadhi, there is neither a person nor a problem that can cause you vexation. From samadhi, you can develop the wisdom of no-self. This is Ch'an enlightenment. To reach enlightenment is to see into your self-nature and be free of mental disturbance and illness. At the point when you are always in this state and do not fall back, you have realized "great enlightenment." Short of that is "small enlightenment." Your old problems may arise after you reach the point of small enlightenment, but you will know how to deal with them. Finally, you should remember that great and small enlightenment aside, merely deciding to meditate is very important and a great step towards your liberation.

Ch'an
Tradition

You may have heard that Ch'an (Zen) Buddhism resembles a religion, but is not truly a religion. Ch'an Buddhism is indeed a religion. Religions require faith, and the
practice of Ch'an cannot be accomplished without faith. Understand, though, that the faith we speak of in the Ch'an
tradition is different from faith as it is conceived in other
religions, which emphasize belief in supernormal beings or
gods distinct from oneself. Ch'an stresses the importance
of having faith in the Dharma, or teachings of the Buddha.
These teachings tell us that everyone has Buddha-nature
and that everyone can attain Buddhahood. Every human
being who truly has faith in the teachings of the Buddha
and follows the principles and methods of practice can become a Buddha.

When we discuss the development of Ch'an in China,
we face difficulties in separating specific concepts shaping
Ch'an from those of Buddhism in general. The fact is that
it is impossible to achieve the highest attainment in
Buddhism without the experience of practice equivalent
to that found in the Ch'an tradition. Buddhism emphasizes
the cultivation and realization of wisdom, which resolves
internal struggles and suffering. But how do we cultivate

wisdom? We rely on the guidance of Buddhist methods similar to those found in Ch'an practice.

Buddhism was first brought to China about one thousand years after Sakyamuni Buddha attained enlightenment and introduced the world to the Dharma. During Buddhism's early period, *dhyana* cultivation was set forth as the primary method of practice. Dhyana cultivation systematically calms the mind which, in turn, catalyzes an understanding of self that generates wisdom. The introduction of this method as an opening to the path of wisdom was important to the transmission of Buddhism to China.

There are many stories in the Ch'an tradition about disciples asking their masters the question, "What did Bodhidharma bring from India to China?" The answers from all the masters appear to be different, but their essential point is the same: Bodhidharma brought nothing to China but himself. He went to China to tell people that everyone has Buddha-nature and that everyone can attain Buddhahood.

When a disciple in one such story asked why, the master replied, "Because it already existed in China." The disciple continued, "If it already existed in China, then why did Bodhidharma have to come?" The master answered, "If he did not come, people in China would not know that Buddha-nature exists in every sentient being." Bodhidharma went to China with nothing but himself to spread the message that everyone has Buddha-nature and that everyone should have faith in it. Before becoming enlightened, you must have faith that you have Buddha-nature.

The Sixth Patriarch, Hui-neng (638-713), probably contributed the most to the development of Ch'an. His teaching can be summarized in the phrase: "No abiding, no thought, no form." You must experience the state of mind to which these phrases refer, realize the Buddha-nature in yourself, and realize as well that even though we speak of Buddha-nature, we can point to no concrete form that gives it shape. Buddha-nature is the essence of emptiness – *sunyata.*

In the *Platform Sutra*, attributed to Hui-neng, the teaching of "no abiding, no thought, no form" was consistent with the essential teaching of the *Diamond Sutra* – emptiness. Thus, we should not mistake Buddha-nature for something concrete or unchangeable, for then Ch'an would be indistinguishable from a formal religion, which emphasizes faith in something external, monolithic and unchanging.

The fourth-generation disciple of the Sixth Patriarch, Master Chao-chou (778-897), had a disciple who asked him the following question: "If all sentient beings are supposed to have Buddha-nature, what about dogs?" The master answered, "*Wu,*" which means no. On the surface, this answer seems to contradict what the Buddhadharma teaches. But we need to understand that Buddha-nature is not concrete or unchanging. This kind of dialogue, which seems paradoxical, contradictory, even nonsensical, became a method of practice called *kung-an* or *hua-t'ou.*

Ch'an encompasses four key concepts: faith, understanding, practice, and realization. Faith belongs to the realm of religion; understanding is philosophical; practice is belief put into action; and realization is enlightenment. Without faith, we cannot understand; without understanding, we cannot practice; and without practice, we cannot realize enlightenment. Together, these four concepts create the doorway we enter to attain wisdom.

We must begin Ch'an practice, then, with faith that all beings have Buddha-nature. We must understand as well that Buddha-nature is not something unchanging and substantial. Even if we begin practicing without fully accepting Buddha-nature, we must have faith in its existence. If we do not have faith, we will not be receptive to the teachings or be able to put them to use. Once we accept the existence of Buddha-nature, however, we should not think of it as a static, concrete entity. If we cling to the idea that Buddha-nature is essentially unchanging, we will think a true Self exists within us. We will embrace that Self, whether we think it false or true, and in so doing obstruct our liberation. We must accept the existence of Buddha-nature, and then abandon it completely, recognizing there is no such thing as Buddha-nature! In this way we can truly experience moving from existence of self-centeredness to non-existence of self-centeredness.

Ch'an practice involves meditation, which can be an uncomfortable, physically painful process. Perhaps this is why a few early Ch'an masters did not encourage sitting meditation. Even the old manuscripts and documents show no evidence of the Sixth Patriarch sitting in meditation either before or after his enlightenment.

The first two generations of masters after the Sixth

Patriarch also deemphasized the importance of meditation, as in the famous story about Ma-tsu (709-788) and his master, Nan-yue (677-744). One day while Ma-tsu was sitting in meditation, Nan-yue used a very skillful method to point out its weakness. He asked Ma-tsu, "What are you doing?" Ma-tsu replied, "I am meditating." Nan-yue asked, "Why?" Ma-tsu responded, "I do it to attain Buddhahood." Nan-yue said nothing, picked up a brick, and started polishing it. Ma-tsu asked, "Why are you doing that?" Nan-yue said, "I'm making a mirror." Ma-tsu thought about it and asked, "How is it possible for a brick to become a mirror?" Nan-yue replied, "If you cannot polish a brick to make it become a mirror, then how can you become a Buddha by meditating?"

This dialogue is still a popular teaching and one of my favorite kung-ans. Does it mean that we need not meditate in order to attain Buddhahood or enlightenment? I have been teaching meditation for many years and have come across quite a few very intelligent people who want to follow the practice used by the Sixth Patriarch Hui-neng and Nan-yue. They do not want to sit in meditation, nor do they want meditation to take too much time or cause pain. To these people, I say, "The ancient Ch'an masters are gone now. Modern Ch'an adherents require meditation practice!"

Prior to the Sixth Patriarch, the Third, Fourth and Fifth Patriarchs all emphasized the practice of meditation. Only the Sixth Patriarch and a few generations of his followers deemphasized such practice. We do know from manuscript records that Ma-tsu's disciple, Pai-chang (720-814), conducted ongoing meditation at his monastery. We may say that enlightenment does not come from meditation, but meditating is nonetheless a necessary step toward liberation. And Ch'an teaching should work in conjunction with meditation practice. With the guidance of a good teacher, strong practice, and Ch'an teachings, enlightenment is not far away.

We can calm the mind only by using a method of meditation. Once the mind is calm, we can reduce the subjective and habitual patterns of self-based notions that cause so much vexation. When we achieve a tranquil or unified state of awareness, it is possible to see just what the self is.

There are essentially two major schools of Ch'an meditation: Lin-chi (Jp. Rinzai), which used the methods of kung-an or hua-t'ou, and Ts'ao-tung (Jp. Soto), which uses the method of silent illumination. Using the methods of either of these schools can lead to enlightenment, and regardless of which one you adopt, you must first be able to relax both body and mind and then bring yourself to a concentrated, unified state of mind. Only at this point can you use the methods of kung-an or hua-t'ou and silent illumination.

You cannot fulfill the process of meditation by reading a couple of phrases in a book. Meditation involves long, sustained practice.

The Origin
of
Ch'an
Practice

Bodhidharma's journey to China occurred more than a thousand years after Sakyamuni's death. Because Indian history contains few records of the interim period, we know relatively little about the origins of Ch'an practice.

We do know stories and legends that describe the origins of Ch'an. Most famous is the account of the transmission of the Dharma to Mahakasyapa, one of the Buddha's chief disciples, who became the First Patriarch in the Ch'an lineage. The story is this: one day during a sermon at Vulture Peak, Sakyamuni Buddha held a flower in his hand in front of the assembly and did not speak. No one seemed to know what this gesture meant, but Mahakasyapa smiled. The Buddha said, "The Treasure of the Eye of the True Dharma, the Wonderous Mind of Nirvana; only Mahakasyapa understands." This event marks the beginning of the Ch'an lineage and the master-to-disciple transmission that continues to this day. This story was unknown to Buddhist history until the tenth-century Sung Dynasty. But we should not doubt the entire lineage of the Ch'an tradition just because of one or many apocryphal stories.

It is more important to investigate Ch'an methods themselves than to become caught up in historical debate.

These methods, still practiced today, are captured in stories about the enlightenment of two of Sakyamuni Buddha's disciples, one very bright and the other quite dull.

The first disciple, Ananda, had a powerful mind and a fabulous memory. However, he never attained enlightenment during Sakyamuni's lifetime. Ananda thought that Buddha would reward his intelligence with enlightenment. It never happened. After Buddha entered nirvana, Ananda hoped Mahakasyapa would help him.

After Buddha's death, Mahakasyapa tried to gather 500 enlightened disciples together in order to collect and record the Buddha's teachings. He could only find 499. Some suggested that he invite Ananda, but Mahakasyapa said that Ananda was not an arhat and therefore was unqualified for the assembly. He said that he would rather not have the gathering at all than allow Ananda's attendance.

But Ananda persisted. Three times he was turned away by Mahakasyapa. Ananda said, "Buddha has entered nirvana. Now only you can help me reach enlightenment!" Mahakasyapa said, "I'm very busy. I cannot be of help. Only you can help yourself." At last, Ananda realized that he had to rely on his own efforts if he wished to attain enlightenment. He went off to a solitary and secluded place. As he was about to sit down, he attained enlightenment! Why? At that moment he relied on no one and dropped all of his attachments.

Another story describes the dim-witted disciple named Suddhipanthaka, or Small Path. He was the most stupid of Buddha's disciples. All except Small Path could remember

Buddha's Teachings. If he tried to remember the first word
of a sutra, he forgot the second, and vice versa. Buddha gave
him the job of sweeping the ground, since he didn't seem
fit to do anything else.

After he had swept the ground for a very long time,
Small Path asked, "The ground is clean, but is my mind-
ground as clean?" At that moment everything dropped
from his mind. He went to see the Buddha, who was very
pleased with his accomplishment, and affirmed that Small
Path had become an arhat.

These are recorded in the early texts as true stories,
but their meaning goes beyond their original context. The
first story illustrates that in practice, knowledge and intelligence do not necessarily guarantee enlightenment. The
second story shows that even a dimwit can attain enlightenment. Sakyamuni Buddha, Mahakasyapa, and Sariputra
were people of great learning. Ch'an, however, has less to
do with great learning than with the problem of the mind
that is filled with attachments. Enlightenment can only be
reached when one's mind is rid of attachments.

It is said that twenty-eight generations of transmissions
occurred from the time of Mahakasyapa to that of Bodhidharma, and that in each case only the patriarch was
involved. However, it is unlikely that the patriarchs alone
received transmission. In China, it is also believed that
from Bodhidharma to the Sixth Patriarch Hui-neng, only
the patriarchs received transmission. We know, however,
that Bodhidharma had two or three disciples, as did the
Second and Third Patriarchs. The belief in single-person

transmission stems from the fact that we only recognize the patriarch as having received the direct transmission.

The Sixth Patriarch, Hui-neng, had many disciples who established many branches and generations. Some of these branches still survive today. Therefore, it is unlikely that there was only single transmission for twenty-eight generations from the time of Sakyamuni Buddha in India to Bodhidharma's passage to China.

I am the sixty-second lineage holder of Ch'an from the Sixth Patriarch Hui-neng and the fifty-seventh generation in the Lin-chi tradition. In the Ts'ao-tung lineage, I am the fiftieth generation descendant of the co-founder, Master Tung-shan (807-869). All the masters before me in this lineage had more than one disciple, but when one traces back one's lineage, it makes it seem that there were no other disciples.

We should turn now from this brief discussion of Ch'an history and transmission to a description of the styles that characterize Ch'an practice. The Fifth Patriarch, Hung-jen (d. 674), had two prominent disciples, Shen-hsiu (605?-706) and Hui-neng. The Shen-hsiu style was based on step-by-step practice. Hui-neng, however, emphasized the practice of no practice. Each lineage has its own rules and methods of practice, but each shares the same goal: free the mind and no problems exist. Ch'an practice does not pick and choose among definitive standards. As long as your mind is at peace, you are fine.

Shen-hsiu used this analogy: Cultivation is like polishing a mirror. Examine and rectify your behavior until the self-nature/mirror is clean. This process continues until purity of mind is achieved. According to Hui-neng, there was no mirror and therefore nothing to dust or polish. This means that original self-nature is clean and pure. There is no need to take anything away, no need to add anything. A Ch'an saying illustrates: "As long as there is nothing in your mind, any direction north, east, south, or west is fine."

Proper understanding is essential to Ch'an. If our cultivation is to bear fruit, we must understand the four components that shape the entrance through practice:

1. Accept karmic retribution: The basic Buddhist doctrine of cause and consequence. Difficulties in this life are the result of past deeds. The natural consequences of causes we have effected in past lives should cause no sadness or anger.

2. Be in accord with conditions: Good fortune and pleasant circumstance are the results of meritorious deeds in past lives. They depend on causes and conditions. When the causes and conditions dissipate, the favorable events will also end. Therefore do not be overly happy or proud when faced with favorable conditions.

3. Practice without seeking: Seeking inevitably results in suffering. Do not seek and you will depart from self-centeredness and gain complete freedom of mind.

4. Practice in accord with Dharma: Realize that the self and all phenomena are inherently empty and pure. This practice is the highest of the four and includes the three mentioned above. It is the practice of "direct contemplation" on emptiness, whereby practitioners engage in

helping others and themselves to the fullest extent, yet do not hold on to notions of self, others and accomplishments. They recognize the emptiness of dharmas – of all phenomena – but do not reject their manifold appearances. Therefore, even though their minds carry no attachments, they still work diligently at whatever needs to be done.

Before you begin practice, enlightenment is your motivation. In fact, you must have motivation if you are to practice. But once you start practice, you must drop your intention to seek enlightenment. Motivation is a form of self-attachment, and if you don't drop attachment, you will never realize enlightenment.

Let us now discuss the Sixth Patriarch Hui-neng's style of "stageless" practice. The *Platform Sutra* emphasizes practice in which, though functioning amidst daily circumstances, regardless of time and place, one's mind is not caught up with notions of virtue and evil, good and bad, right and wrong. The mind is detached from such discriminating thoughts. Such detachment in itself is practice.

The mind usually referred to in the *Platform Sutra* is the fundamental pure mind, which is the equivalent of *prajna* (wisdom), or enlightenment. The central theme in the *Platform Sutra* is "no thought, no form, and no abidance." No thought is non-attachment and no abidance, which means that one does not attach to thought nor abide in thought. Thoughts, responses and memories occur, but the mind does not cling to them.

No thought is the equivalent of no form, which is the characteristic of all physical, mental, or material phenomena that exist within time and space. No form means no fixed appearance or form. No form is one and the same with pure mind, and one and the same as wisdom and enlightenment. These ideas reveal the original true nature of mind or reality, which is not something aquired "after" we use a method to practice. We do not need to fabricate any method to create this enlightened nature. Buddha-nature is already perfect in itself and already present. It is due only to our vexations that we cannot directly experience enlightenment.

Next let's discuss the style of Ch'an practice that gradually lessens vexation and increases wisdom. This practice can be divided into two categories: daily practice and periodic practice. Daily practice involves maintaining regular daily meditation. You meditate for a certain period each day. When not practicing meditation, you deal with people and situations in daily life with a concentrated, content, humble, and grateful mind. I often tell my students to pay attention wherever they are and focus on whatever they are doing at the moment. Live in the present. This, too, is daily practice.

However, daily practice is not enough. You need periodic, concentrated practice as well. Every week, month or year you should set aside time to practice alone, whether it is a day or two, seven days or even a month. Use that block of time to concentrate on nothing but practice. The second kind of periodic practice, group practice, provides a safe, focused environment where practitioners can help each other.

Both kinds of concentrated periodic practice are useful, in that they strengthen your discipline and the diligent use of a method. Without daily practice, however, your vexation and suffering will tend to increase. Your mind will not be peaceful.

I once knew a high-ranking Catholic priest who was always busy running around to different places and conducting numerous activities. I asked him how he managed to maintain his presence of mind without being distracted or being tempted to go back to the secular life, to marry and raise a family. He replied that priests practice spiritual cultivation two to four hours daily. Without this daily practice, it would be difficult for him to remain a priest.

This is why Ch'an emphasizes daily practice. Meditation alone is not enough. You must conduct your daily activities with the same presence of mind that you bring to meditation.

Entering
the
Gate

Ch'an is often referred to as the "gateless gate." The
"gate" is both a method of practice and a path to liberation;
this gate is "gateless," however, which means that Ch'an
does not employ any specific method to help a practitioner
achieve liberation. The methodless method *is* the highest
method. So long as a practitioner can drop his or her self-
centered conscious mind, the gateway into Ch'an will open
naturally. Nevertheless, most people stand outside of the
gate and remain stuck in the idea of enlightenment. Unable to experience enlightenment themselves, they can
only be inspired by the stories of enlightened Ch'an masters. For this reason, many people in China have thought
of Ch'an as something that can only be practiced by young
people with good karmic roots.

In response to people's needs, past Ch'an masters
adapted other forms of practice and invented methods that
made Ch'an more accessible. In fact, we can say that there
is not a single spiritual practice that falls outside of Ch'an
cultivation – so long as it is practiced with the understanding of Ch'an. For example, sitting meditation, or the cultivation of samadhi, is not the final goal of Ch'an practice.

But in order to reach the state of Ch'an, you must have a foundation in samadhi. In fact, the term for sitting meditation in both Chinese (*tso-ch'an*) and Japanese (*zazen*) derive from the words "Ch'an" and "Zen".

In most spiritual traditions of India, the yogis practice dhyana to attain various levels of samadhi; a high level of samadhi is the goal of their practice. Before his enlightenment, Sakyamuni Buddha also practiced this and attained the highest state of samadhi possible at that time. But after years of austere practice as a yogi, he recognized that his realization was incomplete. So he sat under the Bodhi tree, vowing not to rise until he had resolved the question of birth and death, the suffering of samsara. Only after seeing a bright morning star and becoming enlightened did he rise. He had become a Buddha, the primal transmitter of Buddhism in our epoch. The Buddha's enlightenment became the paradigm of tso-ch'an.

With the rise of the Ch'an school, two forms of practice developed. One approach de-emphasized the practice of tso-ch'an. The other placed great emphasis on this practice. Both approaches can lead to enlightenment, the realization of no-self. These Ch'an practices are similar to those of traditional Buddhism, which stresses two practices that lead to liberation. The first practice is called liberation through samadhi. The second is called liberation through wisdom. The latter practice does not cultivate the various levels of samadhi or dhyana, but goes directly into the enlightened state. The practice of liberation through samadhi cultivates the various levels of samadhi or dhyana, until

you reach liberation from samsara. Ch'an follows the path
of liberation through wisdom.

To discuss the two approaches of Ch'an, we must describe what tso-ch'an is. When pre-Ch'an masters practiced,
they mostly used the methods introduced in the early Buddhist scriptures; according to their interpretation, tso-ch'an
referred to sitting methods that led to samadhi. But among
the later masters of Ch'an, tso-ch'an referred to methods of
attaining enlightenment that did not necessarily involve
samadhi as an intermediate or final stage. The same holds
true for the term samadhi. In later usage, the term was conjoined with wisdom.

We should not devalue the traditional cultivation of
meditation practice, which, when practiced properly, can
make our bodies healthy and our minds balanced. With the
practice of tso-ch'an, our minds become less self-centered
and can become much more stable and clear. Furthermore,
the limits of the mind can be stretched to accommodate
insight and wisdom. From the perspective of Ch'an, however, any insight or wisdom that arises within us without
the guidance of Buddhadharma will still bear residual effects of vexation, because our self-centeredness remains.
When we confront adverse situations, perhaps in our relations with people, surroundings, or events, vexation can
arise at any time from this self-centeredness. Needless to
say, pain and suffering invariably follow vexation.

Tso-ch'an focuses on regulating body, breath, and
mind. Regulating the body involves relaxing the body
while sitting in a correct posture. In order to cultivate

physical well-being, however, you really need to regulate all aspects of your life. Besides the sitting posture, you can practice walking meditation, sleeping postures, exercises, and massages. You should also regulate and balance your daily diet, your work habits, and the amount of time you sleep. There must be equilibrium between movement and stillness.

Regulating the breath can help you reach many different levels of practice. Breath and mind are very much connected: you can regulate your mind by regulating your breath, because when your breathing is smooth and stable, your mind becomes stable. Every tradition of spiritual meditation practice, including Taoism, yoga, tantra, and Buddhism, all begin by regulating the breath, for the very simple reason that it is the breath within the body that helps the circulation of energy. This energy, or *ch'i*, in turn maintains the functions of the physical body. When practitioners experience the benefits of the ch'i, they tune into the importance and pleasure of meditation practice.

According to your level of concentration, there can be four levels of breathing:

The first level, nostril breathing, is the shallowest one. Its meaning is just what the name suggests. At this stage, you are breathing through the nostrils about 16 to 18 times per minute.

The second level is called abdominal breathing. As your breathing becomes deeper, although your breath still passes through the nostrils, there are movements of the rising and falling of the abdomen.

The third level is called embryonic breathing. At this stage, the breath no longer passes through the nostrils. Instead, every pore throughout the body is breathing. The whole universe is like the womb of the mother, and your body – the embryo – receives oxygen directly from the environment.

The fourth level is called tortoise breathing. At this stage, oxygen from the external environment is no longer needed. Your metabolism slows down so much that even the heart stops beating. You are in a very deep state of samadhi. The body of the meditator becomes its own small universe. The energy inside the body circulates, supports, and nourishes itself.

Regulating the mind involves learning to be in control of your thoughts. Usually, methods of *samatha* and *vipassana* are used to collect and calm the scattered mind. Traditional methods within Buddhism – counting the breath, following the breath, and contemplating the impurity of the body – help you reach a calm and collected state of mind and body. You can also calm and balance mind and body by practicing prostration, walking meditation, and recitation of the Buddha's name.

The traditional purpose of tso-ch'an practice is to concentrate and unify the mind. When people reach this state, they usually think they are enlightened, or that they have achieved the state of no-self. In reality, whatever they may experience is at most a stage of samadhi. There are eight stages of samadhi; none of them go beyond the state of the unified mind. These states are not the wisdom of emptiness, because attachment to the self still exists even when the mind is unified. In Ch'an the understanding of samadhi is very different.

So what is the meaning of samadhi or *ch'an-ting* in the Ch'an tradition? The *Platform Sutra* of the Sixth Patriarch Hui-neng says: "Externally without any features is *Ch'an*; internally the unscattered mind is *ting*... Not seeing the right and wrong of others . . . moment to moment, one perceives the purity of the intrinsic self-nature." From this description, we see that ch'an-ting goes beyond achieving a unified state of mind. Ch'an-ting aims for the pure wisdom that illuminates any circumstance you might encounter.

Simply put, the obstacle to attaining wisdom is attachment to the self. When you face people, things, and situations, the notion of "I" arises immediately within you. When you attach to this "I," you begin making numerous value judgments.

But how might we define non-attachment? According to Ch'an, non attachment means that when you face circumstances, when you deal with other people, there's no "I" in relation to whatever may appear in front of you. There will be no extra discriminations added to the situation. Things are as they are, vivid and clear. You can respond appropriately and give whatever is needed.

Self-centered attachment rears up most often in situations involving family matters, relationships between men and women, and, not least, money. We confront self-centeredness as well when our social status, opinions, and views are at stake. Finally, practitioners find it very difficult to let go of the accomplishments and experiences they've achieved in their practice. They may be willing to drop everything, but when it comes to the value they place on concepts and views of practice or personal experiences, they cannot let go. Even advanced practitioners are sometimes very arrogant. They believe or affirm that they have experienced and achieved something, and consequently obstruct their liberation. In short, any attachment to circumstances, people, or even practice, will prevent you from ultimate cultivation of wisdom.

Ch'an expressions refer to enlightenment as "seeing your self-nature." But even this is not enough. After seeing your self-nature, you need to deepen your experience even further and bring it into maturation. You should have enlightenment experiences again and again and support them with continuous practice. Even though Ch'an says that at the time of enlightenment, your outlook is the same as that of the Buddha, you are not yet a full Buddha. Therefore, in old China, prior to enlightenment, Ch'an adepts practice very hard. After enlightenment, they would sojourn with various Ch'an masters to refine their understanding and deepen their experience. For only then would they have the "clear eyes" needed to seek out genuine masters and study under them.

Even though the practice of tso-ch'an is engaged before and after enlightenment, Ch'an is not necessarily sitting practice. Therefore, in the *Platform Sutra*, Hui-neng said: "In [my Dharma] gate of tso-ch'an, one should neither hold on to mind nor observe purity. [I do not teach people] to be unperturbed . . . [Though] I know some people teach others to observe their mind and contemplate purity, making the mind unmoving so it gives rise to nothing, these teachers are just deluding others; eventually, people will be so attached to this method as to become insane." Ch'an advocates that samadhi and prajna, or wisdom, are inseparable. Samadhi is the essence of prajna, and prajna is the function of samadhi.

The opening verse of *Faith in Mind*, a poem attributed to Seng-tsan (d.606), the third patriarch of Ch'an in China says, "The Ultimate Path is not difficult, so long as you do not pick and choose." What this means is that finding and attaining the highest Path is not hard. If you can leave behind your discriminating mind, then the Path will naturally manifest in front of you. Why is this so? Because the Path is natural and originally present. It is not something expedient. If the Path can be practiced through fabricated methods, then whatever you practice will not be the genuine Path, but the expedient Path.

When Ma-tsu became a Ch'an master, he advocated that the "ordinary mind" is the Path. Whether you are walking, standing still, sitting, or lying down, everything is Ch'an practice. He taught that the Bodhisattva Path is neither the path of the ordinary people nor of the sages. You should not intentionally practice to gain, nor get involved in what is right or wrong, in grasping and rejecting. This is the practice of what he calls the "ordinary mind."

Although Hui-neng and some other early patriarchs

following him de-emphasized tso-ch'an practice, most great Ch'an masters did practice intensely. For example, in the monastic rules of Ch'an master Pai-chang, the immediate successor of Ch'an master Ma-tsu, there were regulations concerning daily tso-ch'an practice. Even though there were no accounts of how many hours they sat daily, their meditation platforms were built so people could lie down when necessary. From this we can presume that the monks spent most of their time sitting. Practice also guided the monks' daily routines and their work in the community. A famous motto passed down through the generations from Pai-chang's community insists, "A day without work is a day without food." We know from records that the monks supported themselves in part by working in rice fields and chopping up firewood in the mountains.

Actually, this aspect of making your daily work the practice of Ch'an was not something that Pai-chang created. Hui-neng himself also lived his practice. Before meeting the Fifth Patriarch, Hung-jen, Hui-neng chopped firewood for a living. After meeting Hung-jen, he was sent not to the meditation hall, but to the kitchen to grind rice. During his years working in the kitchen, Hui-neng cultivated his mind, teaching himself to maintain a stable and concentrated state of awareness. In doing so, he let go of the ups and downs of emotions and moods. Achieving this clear awareness is important, because only in this mental state will a practitioner have a chance to become enlightened. Of course, practitioners also need correct guiding views. Even before meeting Hung-jen, Hui-neng had experienced an initial enlightenment, which occurred when he overheard someone reciting a verse from the *Diamond Sutra*. From his enlightenment experience, he understood attachment and detachment, as well as the difference between self and no-self. These understandings became his guiding views.

The second approach of Ch'an does advocate the practice of tso-ch'an. This approach *begins* with the traditional view that wisdom and samadhi are different. From this point of view, wisdom is generated from samadhi. According to the Fifth Patriarch Hung-jen's treatise on *The Essentials of Practice*, "To engage in the practice, one must know the principle of the Dharma; guarding the Mind is most crucial." This practice teaches people to guard their innate True Mind. If the True Mind is well guarded, delusion does not arise. When delusion does not arise, the notion of "I" and "mine" will naturally dissolve and fundamental ignorance is extinguished. You then become a Buddha. This is actually a form of samadhi practice.

In *The Song of Samatha*, great master Yung-chia (665-713) talks about "clarity and quiescence, quiescence and clarity." Clarity is *kuan* or contemplation, a practice of contemplating and illuminating your mind. Quiescence is *chih* or cessation, a practice of ending delusionary, scattered thoughts. When using this method, if you reach a point when not a single thought arises, then your mind can become extremely clear and bright. This is when the state of quiescence and clarity, contemplation and cessation are simultaneous. It is possible at this time for enlightenment to manifest.

The two major methods of Ch'an that have come to us
from China are the method of silent illumination and the
method of the kung-an and hua-t'ou. In China, the development of each method's distinct characteristics branched
into two distinct schools of Ch'an Buddhism, namely, the
Ts'ao-tung (Jp. Soto) and Lin-chi (Jp. Rinzai) schools. In
relation to tso-ch'an, these two methods represent the two
different approaches toward Ch'an.

Silent Illumination Ch'an

The term "silent illumination," or *Mo-chao,* is associated with the Sung dynasty Master Hung-chih Cheng-
chueh (1091-1157). However, the practice itself may be
traced back at least as far as Bodhidharma. In his treatise
Two Entries and the Four Practices, Bodhidharma introduced
the concept of entry by principle. The meaning of this concept is very close to the underlying concept of Silent Illumination: "Leaving behind the false, return to the true:
make no discriminations between self and others. In contemplation, one's mind should be stable and unmoving,
like a wall."

In *Faith in Mind,* Seng-ts'an says, "The principle is
neither hurried nor slow – one thought for ten thousand
years." "One thought" refers to the mind which is
completely clear and free from attachment. "Ten thousand
years" is simply a very long time without interruption.
Passages similar to Seng-ts'an's often appear in later
descriptions of silent illumination.

Master Shih-shuang Ch'ing-chu (805-888) was another master whose approach prefigured that of Master Hung-chih Cheng-chueh. He lived on a mountain called Shih-shuang, "stone-frost," for 20 years. His disciples sat continuously, even sleeping in the upright position. In their stillness, they looked so like many dead tree stumps. Thus they were named the "dry wood sangha." Shih-shuang had two famous pieces of advice. One was, "to sit Ch'an, fix your mind on one thought for ten thousand years." The other was, "let yourself be like cold ashes, or dry wood."

Hung-chih, the founder of Silent Illumination Ch'an, studied for a while with Ch'an master K'u-mu. He was called K'u-mu, "dry wood," because when he sat, his body resembled a block of dry wood. In the hands of Hung-chih, this practice evolved into what he called silent illumination. He describes "silent sitting" thus: "Your body sits silently; your mind is quiescent, unmoving. This is genuine effort in practice. Body and mind are at complete rest. The mouth is so still that moss grows around it. Grass sprouts from the tongue. Do this without ceasing, cleansing the mind until it gains the clarity of an autumn pool, bright as the moon illuminating the evening sky."

In another place, Hung-chih said, "In the silent sitting, whatever realm may appear, the mind is very clear to all the details, yet everything is where it originally is, in its own place. The mind stays on one thought for ten thousand years, yet does not dwell on any forms, inside or outside."

How is silent illumination different from what Hui-neng criticizes as "observing mind and contemplating purity?" What Hui-neng refers to is a method of samadhi that lacks wisdom. Or more accurately, samadhi is not a method; it is a consequence, or goal of practice. It has no space, no time, and no sense of environment. Silent illumination differs from samadhi practice in that while it keeps the mind still (the silent aspect), it clarifies the inner as well as the outer states (the illumination aspect). Samadhi is silent but not illuminating. In silent illumination, the mind does not abide anywhere. Nothing, not even samadhi, is dwelt on. In the deep level of silent illumination, the mind is not influenced by or disturbed by the environment. Not being fixed in samadhi, the mind is in a bright state of illumination. This is what the meditator works continually to maintain in silent illumination practice.

To understand silent illumination Ch'an, it is important to understand that while there are no thoughts, the mind is still very clear, very aware. Both the silence (mo) and the illumination (chao) must be there. According to Hung-chih, when there is nothing going on in one's mind, one is aware that nothing is happening. If one is not aware, this is just Ch'an sickness, not the state of Ch'an. So in this state, the mind is transparent. In a sense, it is not completely accurate to say that there is nothing present, because the transparent mind is there. But it is accurate in the sense that nothing can become an attachment or obstruction. At this stage, the mind is without form or feature. Power is present, but its function is to fill the mind with illumination, like the sun, shining everywhere. Hence, silent illumination is the tso-ch'an in which there is nothing moving, but the mind is bright, illuminated.

Kung-an and Hua-t'ou Ch'an

A kung-an is a story of an incident between a master and one or more disciples, which involves an understanding or experience of the enlightened mind. The incident usually, but not always, involves dialogue. When the incident is remembered and recorded, it becomes a "public case," which is the literal meaning of the term. Often what makes the incident worth recording is that, as the result of the interchange, a disciple had an awakening, an experience of enlightenment.

Master Chao-chou was asked by a monk, "Does a dog have Buddha-nature?" to which the master replied, "Wu," meaning nothing. As kung-ans go, this is a basic one, possibly the most famous on record. Here is another kung-an, also involving Chao-chou.

Chao-chou had a disciple who met an old woman on the road and asked her, "How do I get to Mt. T'ai?" She said, "Just keep going!" As the monk started off, he heard the old lady remark, "He really went!" Afterwards, the disciple mentioned this to Chao-chou who said, "I think I'll go over there and see for myself." When he met her, Chao-chou asked the same question and she said the same thing: "Just keep going!" As Chao-chou started off, he heard the old lady say again, "He really went!" When Chao-chou returned, he said to the assembly, "I have seen

through that old lady." What did Chao-chou find out about
the old lady? What is the meaning of this lengthy and
obscure kung-an?

Around the time of the Sung dynasty (960-1276),
Ch'an masters began using recorded kung-ans as a subject
of meditation for their disciples. The practitioner was re-
quired to investigate the meaning of the historical kung-
an. In his attempts to penetrate the meaning of the kung-
an, the student has to abandon knowledge, experience, and
reasoning, since the answer is not accessible to these methods. He must find the answer by *ts'an kung-an*, by "investigating the kung-an." This requires his sweeping from his
consciousness everything but the kung-an and eventually
generating the "doubt sensation," which is a strong sense
of wonder and an intense desire to know the meaning of
the kung-an.

Closely related, but not identical to the kung-an, is the
hua-t'ou. A hua-t'ou, literally, "head of the spoken word,"
is a question that a meditator asks him or herself. "What is
Wu?" or "Who am I?" are commonly used hua-t'ous. In the
hua-t'ou practice, the meditator devotes his full attention
to repeatedly, incessantly, asking the question. The kung-
an and the hua-t'ou methods are similar in a sense that the
meditator tries to arouse the great doubt sensation in order
to eventually shatter it and awaken to enlightenment.

Ch'an master Ta-hui Tsung-kao (1089-1163) was one
of the greatest advocates of hua-t'ou practice. From his
record of sayings, he maintained that tso-ch'an was very
necessary to settle the wandering mind and bring about

samadhi. It is only then that the student can effectively use the kung-an or hua-t'ou. Even though kung-an and hua-t'ou practice can be done while walking, standing, or even lying down, its fundamental basis is still tso-ch'an.

If through tso-ch'an a student's mind becomes very peaceful and stable, the application of the kung-an or hua-t'ou may cause the rise of the great doubt. This doubt is not the ordinary doubt of questioning the truth of an assertion. It is the doubt that arises out of *ts'an Ch'an*, investigating Ch'an. The resolution of the kung-an or hua-t'ou hinges on nurturing the great doubt. Because the nature of the question cannot be resolved by logic, he must begin by continually returning to the question, and in the process clear his mind of everything except the great doubt.

Eventually, this accumulated "doubt mass" grows bigger and bigger, and can disappear in one of two ways: Due to lack of concentration or energy, the meditator will not be able to sustain the doubt, and it will dissipate. Or the meditator can persist until his doubt is like a "hot ball of iron stuck in his throat." In this case, the doubt mass will eventually disappear in an explosion.

If the explosion has enough energy, it is possible that the student will experience Ch'an, see Buddha-nature, become enlightened. If not, there will probably still be some attachment in his mind. It is necessary and important for a master to confirm his experience, since the student, with rare exceptions, cannot do that himself. Even as great a master as Ta-hui did not penetrate sufficiently into his first experience. His master Yuan-wu (1063-1135) told him,

"You have died, but you have not come back to life." He was confirmed on his second experience. So what is a true experience? It takes an adept master to tell. If he is not a genuine master, he won't know the difference between a true and false enlightenment .

Even though Ch'an talks about "non-reliance on words and language," guiding concepts and views are still very important in the course of your practice. Even though you should not become attached to words and language, you still need them to get the message of Buddhadharma. In Ch'an, this idea is called "borrowing the teachings to awaken the principle."

Had Hui-neng never heard the verse from the *Diamond Sutra*, "Give rise to mind while abiding nowhere," he would not have experienced his initial awakening. Had he only held on to those words he heard, he would not have attained enlightenment. Ch'an takes the teachings as "the finger pointing to the moon." If there were no finger, no one would know where the moon is. If everyone just held on to the finger, and did not see where it pointed, then the finger would be useless. But if people truly see the moon, the finger is no longer necessary.

It is because people cannot calm their minds that the practice of tso-ch'an is needed. Even though people engage in practice, they may still be unable to maintain concentration and stability. So continual practice of tso-ch'an is needed. We can say that even though Ch'an is not necessarily the result of sitting practice, by engaging in sitting practice, the power of samadhi generated will be a good foundation for enlightenment. However, if your practice is very loose and lacks correct guiding views, you will never enter the gate of Ch'an.

Daily Living

The study and practice of Ch'an Buddhism develops an understanding of certain principles of non-attachment. One principle is that a Ch'an practitioner does not dwell on his or her learning or accomplishments. If you've written a book, let go of your efforts and forget the contents. The book is done. It's gone. Just forget about it and move on. Another principle is that while you should have money in the bank and money in your pocket, you should have no money in your head. Both principles emphasize the importance of maintaining an empty mind. Some people believe the opposite: They obsess about their past efforts and accomplishments; or their minds are filled with money, but their pockets are turned inside out and their bank accounts register a zero balance.

If I am giving a lecture and the topic is Ch'an, then there's no need for preparation. If I am to speak about my scholarly research, however, then I prefer to have advance warning; learned words have limitations, but in certain situations they are unavoidable. True Ch'an teaching does not rely on words, but on practice and direct experience.

When we say that Ch'an does not rely on words, we mean that Ch'an does not depend on what has been spoken or written in the past. If we recognize that there is no need to believe even the words of Sakyamuni Buddha, we can approach Ch'an unencumbered by what we have heard and what we have read. Other religions and schools of philosophy wrestle with considerable verbiage. Ch'an advocates throwing everything away. When you practice, leave the past behind – what you have read, heard and experienced.

Recently, when I spoke about this principle of letting go and leaving behind, someone said, "It sounds scary to throw away your whole past and totally discard everything you know." I am not really advocating that you return to a vegetative state, in which your head resembles a dried pumpkin. We must learn, but we should not cling to what we have learned. We don't want learning in our heads when we practice.

Most of us, however, find it difficult to let go of cherished concepts and views.

Once I slept at a professor's house. In the morning, when we gathered for breakfast, his wife asked me, "Did you sleep well? Did anything bother you?" I said, "I slept quite well." I told them that no place in the world is free from noise and disturbance. She added that no matter where we are or what we do, our minds are always buzzing with self-created problems. This is true: we are most disturbed by what goes on in our heads and not by what goes on around us.

Our minds are full of thoughts: impressionistic, illusory tangles of the past, present, and future. For the most part, our thoughts consist of worrying that we cannot get what we want when we want it, and that we cannot get rid of what displeases us when we are displeased.

It might seem that some people always get what they want. Imagine a playboy. Perhaps he has three girlfriends he can telephone on any given night. Even though he can call whichever girlfriend he wants, he still has to choose one of the three. Can he call all three at the same time? There are limits to everything.

You might think that it's easy to get rid of what you don't want, but this is not necessarily so. Many people get married, decide that they want to be single again, and then discover that dissolving a marriage is no easy task.

When we make decisions, we usually connect the past, present, and future, a process fraught with contradictions. I don't bother to go through this process. I'm engaged with a long list of activities and have many disciples in Taiwan and in the United States. I am always busy. Nevertheless, I am never disturbed by my obligations and responsibilities. People ask me how I manage to deal with my work; I tell them that I don't put myself in the way of what I do. There is nothing that I wish to do or not do for personal gain or preservation. I do what I have to do with all my heart. I do not do what is not permitted me, what is unnecessary, and what I am unable to do.

Does this mean that I constantly change direction, try one thing, abandon it, and then try something else? No, because a central purpose underlies all my actions. In everything I do, I try to maintain the attitude of a bodhisattva who benefits others as much as possible. If my work for others benefits me as well, that's fine, but self-sacrifice is sometimes needed. Because I maintain such an attitude, I have few vexations.

Understand that the willingness to sacrifice yourself is really the mark of a saint, and that most of us are neither ready nor able to maintain such an attitude. Do not burden yourself with overwhelming, unrealistic demands. Do what you can with the abilities you possess right now. Don't think you have to be a saint and perform miraculous deeds. It is Confucianism that advocates striving after sagehood or sainthood. And though Buddhism does advocate the bodhisattva ideal, that ideal should be adopted only by those who are ready. Everything comes in its time. To be taken for a bodhisattva when you have not truly attained this state is to invite serious problems.

I sometimes come across people who treat me as if I were a great master. To such people, I say, "I'm sorry to disappoint you, but please don't take me for a saint. Otherwise you will end up causing both of us harm." Why would anyone want to add to his or her suffering by posing as someone else's ideal, as someone else's illusion? Most often our suffering derives from unrealistic demands that we make on ourselves or that others make upon us.

Regardless of our nationality or culture, Ch'an offers all of us ways to deal with the suffering we impose on ourselves. Many people feel that Ch'an is an exotic product of the Orient that is of no use to the West. A similar attitude arose in China when Buddhism was first introduced there.

Many Chinese thought that it was a foreign imposition that was unsuited and unadaptable to Chinese culture. But remember the story I told earlier. Bodhidharma did not bring Buddhadharma from India to China. The Dharma was always present in China, just as it is present any and everywhere else.

Bodhidharma also said that anyone can become a Buddha and that everyone has Buddha-nature. But none of us automatically realize Buddha-nature. So in order to help us attain this realization, Bodhidharma gave us two methods. The first is the method of principle. The second is the method of practice.

When you use the method of principle, you find there is nothing to talk about and nothing to do. You don't use logic and there is no need to practice. You simply make your mind the same as a wall. This wall is transparent and does not move. Nonetheless, you can hang things on it and write on it. The wall itself, however, does not change. Your mind may contain knowledge and experience, but remains unaffected by them. In reality, your mind is empty of everything, just as the substance of the wall is neither enlarged nor reduced by what is hung upon it.

When the mind is confused, you believe that what is stored in it is you. You continually try to take some things out and put other things in, which only increases mental motion and confusion. The mind is strange: When you have no use for something stored in it, the something comes out and gets in the way. Conversely, when you need something from your mind, it often happens that this something refuses to emerge.

This afternoon a man forgot what he wanted to say to me. His thoughts were hiding from him. Why?

If your mind is calm and cool, you won't need to search anxiously for information. With a calm mind, what you need will be available. If you find yourself at a loss, it is because your mind is spinning with craving and distress. When your mind is like a wall, useful but unmoving, then it is like the mind of the Buddha.

Can you make your mind like a wall? Can you take all your past knowledge and experiences and lock them in a storehouse? Can you prevent their escape? Who among you thinks that they can do that?

We often meet people who talk constantly. Sometimes there is nothing left for us to do but tell them to shut up. That may be easy. But what happens when it is your mind that you are trying to quiet? Are you able to tell your mind to silence your wandering thoughts?

In order to help us achieve a silent, unmoving mind, Bodhidharma gave us the second method, that of practice. He divided the method of practice into four stages (see Chapter on *The Origin of Ch'an Practice*).

The first stage deals with the recognition of suffering. You see that your problems and the difficulties that befall you stem from your previous karma, that everything existing in the present has its origin in some other place and some other time. You may not be able to know this origin. What has brought us and everything around us to this present moment is rooted in innumerable past lives. But most of us cannot look deep into the past, and there is no way for us to prove the existence of past lives. Even in this life there is much we are unable to remember. When we are confronted by unpleasantness and unhappiness in the present, we should know that our difficulties stem from what we have done in the past. We may be unable to perceive the exact cause, but we should understand that the origin is in ourselves and accept the consequences that we now confront.

Does this unconditional acceptance mean that the Ch'an approach is passive or negative? Not at all. If we understand that our past has lain the groundwork for our present suffering, we can see that the here and now is the groundwork for the future. We can lay down a new cause to counteract our present suffering and immediately put ourselves on a more positive course. In laying down new causes, we pay back debts that we have accrued in our past.

It is important to understand that this paying back consists of acting properly in the present moment with what we have at hand. It does not mean surrendering. If this building burst into flames, there would be cause for the fire. What would we do? Would we attempt to douse the flames? Or would we sit down and try to figure out how the fire started? There's no need to concern ourselves with the reason. What we must do is to put out the flames. When we have done everything that is humanly possible, only then do we unequivocally accept the consequences without complaint.

In the second stage, we develop the awareness that what we find good or pleasant is also the result of causes in the past, and we don't get caught up in feelings of satisfaction. We don't take good fortune as a sign of our own specialness or greatness. We don't let such things add to a sense of self. After all, when something good happens to us, we are simply experiencing the consequences of the hard work we have done in the past. It is as if we are withdrawing money from the bank. And what is so wonderful about withdrawing money from our account?

We must realize that happy events are not all that they seem. Some people still find ways to be unhappy in pleasant circumstances. Many of those with wealth, power and position are not necessarily happy. Even a simple, common event such as boy meeting girl may not create happiness for all parties involved. This is not to say that they will necessarily be unhappy. But good fortune and happy occurrences should not lead to feelings of pride or self-satisfaction. A lot of people forget themselves when they meet with success.

There is a story in China about a beggar who won a lottery. He had the winning ticket secreted in a bamboo walking stick. When he found out that he had won the prize, he was so overjoyed that he resolved then and there that he would never again have anything to do with begging. In a burst of exultation he threw his old clothes and all his meager possessions into a nearby river. Unfortunately, the walking stick was one of the discarded items. Too late, he watched the stick and his new life float downstream.

A Ch'an practitioner should maintain an attitude of equanimity. If the money comes, it comes. If it goes, it goes. Neither circumstance should create wild fluctuations in the mind.

By the third stage, the practitioner maintains an attitude of not seeking. Of course, whether you live in the East or in the West, it makes sense that nothing can be accomplished if you don't set out to accomplish it. Normally, we have desires and goals we strive to attain. Goals and desires are natural sources of motivation. Often, however, we find ourselves unable to attain what we seek.

A Chinese saying: If you have the intention of planting a flower, the flower will not blossom. But a willow will flourish even if no one plants it.

Most young people have lots of ideas about what they want to do with their lives. They may have some career in mind even in their pre-school years. When they reach junior high school, do their goals change? And in high school? Their first year in college?

A professor I know has a Ph.D. in philosophy. He also has a master's degree in music, and he's now studying massage and physical therapy. Even though he has applied himself to a number of diverse subjects, I don't think that this has been a problem for him at all. He is embarking on his own path.

Imagine a house with many entrances. You may enter from the east or the west side. You can take a helicopter and enter the house from above. You may go in one way, dislike what you see, and then try another entrance.

Regardless of which door you use as an entry, what you see when you get into the interior of the house is the same. But if you stubbornly stick to one entrance and can't get past the door, that is a problem. You may see other people going in through that door, but if you can't, you have to find another way in. It doesn't matter what others think of you.

Not seeking anything, there is no single goal to attain. Nonetheless, we must work hard. Without hard work, life is meaningless. We need to work. We need motivation to accomplish everyday tasks. But in terms of spiritual cultivation, keeping a specific goal in mind is itself an obstacle to the accomplishment of the goal. Ordinary aims can be achieved by desire and direct effort, but the highest goal cannot be approached in this way.

If, for example, you practice to achieve enlightenment, you will find your goal moving farther and farther away from you. True enlightenment means liberation, both from constraints imposed by the self and those imposed by the external world. Seeking, even if it is for enlightenment, is just another constraint.

Each stage of practice reaches for a progressively higher level of awareness. The first two stages, those of recognizing suffering and letting go of satisfaction, are fairly easy to carry out. The third stage, that of not seeking, poses more of a problem. Few can fully integrate this stage into their practice.

Finally, we come to the fourth and final stage of practice, in which you simply do whatever should be done.

Whatever you need of me, I do. Someone who has only reached the third stage may do a task well, but there may be some negativity in his attitude. But by the fourth stage of practice, the practitioner manifests positive, forthright action.

I once met a young man who had wanted to become a lawyer from the time he graduated from high school. As it turned out, he was unable to pass the entrance exam, so he eventually studied library science instead. At first he was quite disappointed in his choice. After he graduated, he went to France to do research on the French library system. Eventually, he received his Ph.D. in library science. Then he was invited back to Taiwan because there are very few Ph.D.'s in library science there, and they needed somebody for the central library. He came to me for advice and I quoted a Chinese saying to him: "Once you board the pirates' boat, be a pirate." I told him to go all the way with library science. He came back from France and thanked me. Things turned out quite well for him, probably better than if he had become a lawyer.

Strive to be your best in whatever situation you find yourself; don't act out some illusion you fear or crave. When things change, change with them. With this attitude, your life will run smoothly and your vexations and troubles will be few.

Knowing
and
Doing

Practice can be divided into regular periodic practice and daily practice; regular periodic practice can be further divided into individual and group practice. Individual practice is for those who maintain a stable practice that uses a specific method. They set aside time every week, month or year to practice on their own. Group practice is similar, except that it is done with others. Seven-day Ch'an retreats, sutra recitations, and repentance ceremonies are examples of group practice. Serious practitioners should engage in regular periodic practice a few times each year.

Let me concentrate now on daily practice. There are two types of daily practice: fixed practice and ordinary activity practice. In fixed practice, you designate certain times each day to sitting, prostrating, reciting or reading sutras, or performing morning and evening services. Fixed practice requires that you set up a regular schedule and adhere to it.

Fixed practice has a definite structure, but how do you practice when working, commuting, entertaining, socializing and so on? In fact, you can practice in all these situations. Usually, when people think about practice, meditation or studying Buddhadharma comes to mind, but Ch'an stresses that you should take advantage of all moments, whether you are practicing in a structured manner or following a daily routine. Any situation or environment is simply another opportunity to practice.

In the *Avatamsaka Sutra*, there is a famous chapter, in the form of a gatha (verse), from which the Three Refuges were taken. This chapter speaks of all the human activities: eating, sleeping, walking, resting, talking, and so forth. Its essence is that in all activities, we should practice Bodhi mind, which makes the welfare of sentient beings our foremost concern.

A person on the Bodhisattva Path should think of helping sentient beings. This is the first of the Four Great Bodhisattva Vows. If you can consistently think of the welfare of other sentient beings, compassion will naturally arise in your thoughts and actions. The greatest problems a practitioner faces are arrogance, greed and anger, which manifest when we place ourselves ahead of others.

If we forego pride and put others ahead of ourselves, we will realize that attainment is possible only with the help of sentient beings. Only through interacting with others can we live and grow in knowledge and ability. It is also wrong to expect gratitude when we do something for others. Indeed, we should thank sentient beings for giving us a chance to practice Bodhi mind and cultivate merit and virtue.

Without sentient beings, a bodhisattva cannot attain Buddhahood. For this reason, we should be grateful to everyone. If we have not helped them, we should make it a point to do so; if we feel we have done something for them, we should be thankful for such opportunities. In any case, we should be grateful. Such an attitude will transform our habitual patterns of thinking and prevent a great deal of pride and arrogance.

But greed, anger, arrogance, and hatred arise in our minds all too easily. Greed arises from wanting more of what we already have and wanting what other people have. To be miserly is a product of greed: what is my own I am unwilling to give away.

Anger comes from not having things the way we want them to be; it can arise when something or someone blocks our way. Envy and hate come when we cannot get what we want. Hatred can also arise when someone is different from us, or too much like us. Arrogance, which grows out of pride, can arise if we think we possess some kind of spiritual attainment or other ability. These feelings come up because our self-centeredness causes vexation after vexation to come into our lives. If we let vexations arise without checking them, then we are not practicing. If we can put sentient beings before ourselves, our self-centeredness will lessen.

For example, one Thanksgiving eve I asked my editor to come to the Ch'an Center and spend the night and part of Thanksgiving Day doing some editing and paperwork. He agreed, and that is good. If he had been very self-centered, he might have said no. But the situation was more complex than it might seem. By working at the Center during a holiday, he may be helping some people, but hurting his family. For this reason I apologized to him and his family and said that I hoped his wife would not be upset.

In all our actions, we should reflect on whether our intentions are beneficial to others. Likewise, when negative feelings arise in us, we should reflect on them, to see if they are harmful to others. In this way, we will check ourselves before we act; if we put other sentient beings before ourselves, those selfish feelings will not arise as much.

It is difficult for most of us to think about benefiting sentient beings all the time. Sentient beings include people and animals, but in this case I am putting the emphasis on humans. For example, if a spouse works hard at a job all day, he or she may be in a bad mood upon returning home. On the other hand, if the other spouse has been housekeeping all day, he or she may also be in a bad mood. Two people in bad moods usually spells trouble.

But, if one of the two is mindful enough to perceive that the other may also have had a bad day, he or she will be more attentive, patient, tolerant, and considerate. Fewer problems are likely to arise. Proper practice includes thinking less about yourself and more about others. Cultivating such an attitude is the beginning of compassion.

On one of my retreats, three women shared a room. One complained to me that one thing she hated was snoring, and both of her roommates were snoring their heads off. I said, "Maybe you snore sometimes, too." She said, "I would rather die than snore!" If she could accept the idea that she herself was capable of snoring, she would probably have more consideration for those who do snore.

I told her a story: Once when I was a novice monk I spent a night in the same room with two masters. Both snored, one in a loud, roaring tone and the other in a lower but wheezy tone. It annoyed me. I felt like poking them, but then they might have awakened and found themselves unable to fall asleep again. I decided against that idea. Instead, I imagined that the wheezer was a frog croaking in a marsh and that the other was a tiger roaring in the jungle. On the right a frog, on the left a tiger, right a frog, left a tiger, frog, tiger, frog, tiger . . . and eventually I fell asleep. I remembered that ancient masters could enter samadhi just by listening to the sound of the wind or flowing water. I thought that if it could be done with wind and water, it could also be done with snoring! Perhaps I wouldn't enter samadhi, but at least I'd fall asleep.

Being considerate of others is as much a form of practice as meditation is. Do not only think of yourself; and when you are thinking of yourself, at least do the right thing. How do you know what is right? First, base your decisions and judgments on the teachings of Buddhadharma. If you are not sure whether something is right or wrong or good or bad, then try to determine if it accords with Buddhist teachings and precepts. If it does, then go ahead and do it. If it does not, refrain from doing it. Use Buddhist teachings as your guideline. Second, use society's laws, ethics, morals and customs as a guideline. If your intentions accord with them, then you're probably not off track. Use common sense. You can also ask your Dharma teacher for advice.

Be aware of your changing mental and physical conditions. See how they affect your thoughts, words and actions. For instance, if we are unhealthy or physically hurt, we usually end up in a bad mood. The whole world looks ugly when you are in a bad frame of mind. During these times everything and everyone seem to be lacking. It is easy for anger and hatred to arise. Despite this, from moment to moment, and with everyone you encounter, try to give rise to feelings of gratitude.

Greedy people are usually unaware of their own greed. The same is true for people filled with anger, arrogance, or pride. But sooner or later, practitioners will recognize that they have been greedy, angry, or arrogant. At that time, they should practice repentance. If you can do this every time, you will recognize that these feelings, these non-virtuous mental states, arise less and less.

You repent because you realize that these mental states result from your strong attachment to self. Of course, you must use your self-centeredness to repent, but afterward, the degree of your self-centeredness should lessen. If the situation allows, it is best to repent in front of a Buddha statue. While bowing or prostrating, you should reflect on the things you thought or said or did that were wrong. When you become aware of your wrongdoing, acknowledge your errors and vow not to repeat that behavior. Likewise, whenever something good happens or someone is kind to you, make a conscious effort to feel grateful.

In the monastery in Taiwan, I tell my students to use two sentences in their daily lives. Whenever they meet or receive help from anyone, they should say, "Amitabha Buddha, thank you." They are not directing their thanks to Amitabha Buddha. Their thanks are directed to the person who helped them, but their practice is to recite the name of Amitabha Buddha. For others, saying thank you is enough.

The second sentence, spoken when aware of a wrong action, is, "I'm sorry." To say "thank you" is gratitude and to say "I'm sorry" is repentance. If people can truly hold these two attitudes in their minds and act on them, then they will experience few vexations. If you can do this with genuine concern for sentient beings, then compassion will arise.

To summarize: Be mindful of the welfare of sentient beings. Remind yourself not to be self-centered; repent wrong actions; and feel grateful to others. What I have described, is, in fact, daily practice. If you consistently strive to hold these ideas in you and incorporate them into daily life, you are doing daily practice. At the same time, it is important to continue to meditate so as to be more aware of your mental state. If you are scattered and lack the discipline to cultivate self awareness, you will not see negative feelings arising. If you use meditation as an underlying discipline, you will be more mindful of your actions, intentions, feelings, moods, and thoughts.

Being mindful of your behavior is a tricky business. You should not set up an objective observer in your mind that monitors your intentions, thoughts, words and actions. Doing so will only make you tense and tired. With meditation you will gradually cultivate an inner stillness, so that in any situation, you will not get too excited or emotional. If your mind is relatively peaceful, you will naturally be more aware of your thoughts, and you will know what to say and do. You won't lose control.

When you are controlled by your emotions and impulses, you are in fact out of control, which leads you to say and do things before you think about the consequences. This is how trouble starts. This is how vexations arise for yourself and for others.

Therefore, try to stay peaceful, and exercise restraint in your words and actions. This comes gradually, from regular sitting, from being mindful during your daily practice, and from using Buddhadharma to guide your behavior.

On the other hand, if you are always watching yourself like a critic, you'll drive yourself crazy, or at the least, make yourself miserable. Constant internal surveillance prevents you from functioning smoothly. If piano players always watched themselves play, they wouldn't be able to make music.

Exercising compassion can also be a complicated process. For instance, how should you deal with the impoverished people you pass every day on the streets of the city? This is a difficult question to answer because every situation is different. It depends on who you are, what you can do, how much you have to give. If you are poor and have no money, then you cannot do much. Perhaps you can help an individual person here and there: give food to a homeless family or clothing to someone dressed in rags. If you have money, power, or influence, then you can do more. Perhaps you can help to create a better society and environment. But you must remember that no matter what kind of help you give, there will be those who don't care, who won't listen, and who will not change. When you abide by Buddhist standards, you do what you can. You do your best.

If we merely use money to help these people, the help will be minimal. Our financial resources are limited. Besides, money will not help them in a fundamental way. We have to figure out how we can better the environment and help these people improve the karma that has led them to where they are now. We have to help them understand the principle of cause and consequence, so that they will better understand their situation. In this way we can help them in a fundamental way. Buddhism takes the long view and concerns itself with fundamental issues. As practitioners, we cannot dwell only on short-term solutions. We have to dig beneath the surface. To do this we have to think about how we can spread the Buddhadharma.

To some this work may sound unrealistic. Let's face facts: many of these people are already too far gone to listen to explanations concerning the ways they can change their lives. Even if these people believed in future lifetimes, they are more likely thinking about today and tomorrow, not about years down the road. And they don't want to know about their root problems. They want food, clothing, shelter, drugs, medicine. These people want immediate help. So, what should you do? Should you become a street-corner evangelist and preach Buddhadharma to passers-by?

No, you should not evangelize. That is not the Buddhist way. It will only bring more problems – for you, for others, for Buddhism in general. The best approach is to practice Buddhadharma. If you live it, then you don't have to preach. Buddhadharma will flow from you naturally. If you are of a mind to give, the giving will come naturally. Those who have affinity with you will benefit. This is helping of the highest order. You don't have to evangelize. If you live the Buddhadharma, people will come to you.

Then, there is the other side of the coin. Suppose you work in a dog-eat-dog business. How do you deal with competition with other businesses? It is your job to outdo the competition. Isn't this causing your competitors to suffer? But if you helped your competitors it would mean losing your own job or business. How should you act in these circumstances?

Honest competition is not necessarily evil. It depends on your attitude. In what way are you competitive? The correct attitude is to strive forward and, at the same time, wish your competition to strive forward as well. It's like a swim meet. I do my swimming and you do yours. We don't try to knock each other dead and then go ahead. We encourage a true competitive spirit. This is healthy. It encourages us to perform at higher levels.

An environment of mutual motivation is a healthy environment. In any arena of competition, someone inevitably gets ahead and someone inevitably falls behind.

Indeed, some fall so far behind they cannot make their way back. That area of competition, then, is not for them. They need to switch to another field. That's neither your fault nor your concern. People who fail in one area will survive, and they may go on to succeed in another area. If you work in a dog-eat-dog or unethical business, however, you should consider getting another job. Your livelihood should accord with your sense of Buddhadharma.

Some people are frightened by the bodhisattva ideal. "How can I constantly think of the benefit and welfare of sentient beings?" they ask. The ideal seems to burden them, almost as if it were the greatest vexation of all. But to someone who understands the teachings of Buddhadharma, especially the principle of causes and conditions, the bodhisattva ideal is not burdensome. As you try to help others, remember that sentient beings have their own causes and conditions, their own merit and virtue, their own karma. You cannot change them. You cannot take on other people's karma.

For example, a while back about eighty of us went to India. In Nepal, an older woman in the group was knocked down by a water buffalo and broke her leg. In spite of her handicap, she insisted on continuing with the group. She said, "I want to go on, even if it kills me!"

I said, "If you really want to die, you're better off in Taiwan. If you come with us, the whole group will suffer. As a Buddhist, you should understand karma. That you got knocked down by this buffalo could mean that you owed the buffalo something from a previous life, perhaps your own life; but because you were on a pilgrimage, you only suffered a broken leg. That is your karma. If you insist on continuing the trip, you will be a burden to the whole group, and you will only be creating more bad karma for yourself." Hearing this, she decided to return to Taiwan.

The key word is "*try.*" Of course you should not do anything that would harm others, but you also should try to help. Whether or not you truly help them is another story, and it really isn't your concern. And don't forget what I said earlier. Don't do anything that will make you feel tense, tired or miserable. If you whip yourself all the time, you will be of no use to others or to yourself. Be as mindful as you can. With meditation as a supporting discipline and the Buddhadharma as your guideline, compassion will grow naturally. Do the best you can, but don't push too hard.

Now I'd like to talk a little about karma. To a large degree, karma depends on the intention behind your words or actions. What if you kill a sentient being without knowing it? Suppose you are driving down a dark street at night and a cat runs under the car before you can react. Is karma created? First, you were riding the car by choice. Second, that situation came about because of causes and conditions and because of your karma and the cat's karma. Therefore, karma is created; but the karma is lighter than if you had killed the cat on purpose.

Anything you do with volition creates karma. Random thoughts, for instance, do not create karma. Only thoughts that arise with volition create karma. Such karma is also lighter than karma created by words and actions. Even productive thoughts of practice, your method and the Dharma create karma, but here the karma created is good karma.

Some people mistake intuition for non-discrimination. Unenlightened people can, to varying extents, rely on their intuition. By intuition, I mean knowing, saying and doing things in a direct way, without relying much on the thought process. With a truly non-discriminating mind, there are no vexations. With the mind of intuition, vexations can still arise from the subconscious. A mind of intuition can be cultivated and strengthened with meditation. It is not enlightenment, but it is a good state of mind.

In all cases, however, whether you are cultivating mindfulness, compassion, intuition, or wisdom, you must practice. But, here you are, living in a fast-paced, schedule-filled world. How do you practice when there is not enough time to sit because of a hectic schedule or other obstacles?

During your busy day, try to find little bits of time to sit and relax and clear your mind. You don't need to sit on a cushion, and you don't have to practice for thirty minutes or an hour. Take three or five minutes here and there to sit: at your desk, in a car or bus or train. You can do this anywhere and anytime. Relax your body and mind. Breathe. Settle your mind. Let your mind and body refresh themselves.

Part Two

The
Reality
of
Ch'an
Practice

Some people say that mountain
climbers are really wasting their time.
They have nothing better to do so they
climb mountains, tire themselves out,
and come back with nothing to show
for it. Yet a person who climbs a tall
mountain sees the world and
experiences nature in a very different
way from someone who never leaves
his own front door. Genuine mountain
climbers do not struggle up great
precipices for the glory of it. They
know that glory is only a label given by
others. A true climber climbs for the
experience of climbing. And this is an
experience no one can have without
setting a foot on the mountain path. If
there is any purpose in Ch'an, we may
say it is to discover the nature of the
self. Those who make this effort
discover something sublime. They do
not strive for glory and praise from
others. Rather, they do the work for
themselves.

Those who take up the study of Buddhism before their views have expanded are subject to fears and doubts. They doubt the method and whether they can reach the objective. Like those who have narrow views and only see what is in front of their eyes, their perspective is shallow and limited.

Wh8at is known and what is seen are
more important than what you do.
Knowing and seeing refer to practice
that is in accord with what the Buddha
knows and sees. Practice is important,
but that which the Buddha knows and
sees is even more important. Without
the guidance of the Buddha's
experience, people would not be
practicing Buddhadharma correctly.

Over the years I have met many people who lack faith, who reach a certain point in their practice and find they can go no further. They may have partial faith; for instance, they may have confidence in themselves but no trust in the method. Or they may put all their faith in the method and mistrust the teacher. Some people may trust the teacher but doubt the level they can actually reach with Ch'an practice. Their doubt prevents them from having a deep experience.

Disciples who take refuge in the
Three Jewels should have complete
faith in them as a vehicle and a place
of refuge throughout their lives. Then
they must have faith that their
Buddha-nature is not different from
that of Buddhas and bodhisattvas.

The *Avatamsaka Sutra* says: "Faith is the origin of the Path and the mother of all merit and virtue. It nurtures all wholesome roots in sentient beings." Those who do not have faith in others will not be able to stand on their own. Those who are always suspicious will be lonely.

For lay practitioners, the foundation of Buddhist practice is the five precepts: no killing, no stealing, no sexual misconduct, no lying, and no alcohol or drugs. On the one hand, the five precepts serve as a shield that protects practitioners, ensuring the purity of their lives and minds so they can continue to practice safely and steadily. On the other hand, upholding the precepts is nurturing our compassion toward ourselves, those around us and our society.

The two greatest principles of the Buddhadharma are the belief in karma and the recognition of cause and condition. Be careful not to create causes that lead to the Three Evil Paths. Instead, cultivate the causes for enlightenment. Upholding the five precepts and striving to be good creates a better environment for future practice. Even those who are liberated must abide by karma, for they still live in the phenomenal world.

One who knows karma or cause and consequence will practice benevolence toward others. One who can clearly recognize cause and condition can shatter the wall of self-attachment and biased views. According to the Mahayana Bodhisattva Path, only by employing the two principles can we engage with true faith and practice.

You must be a good lay practitioner in order to become a good monk. If you are not doing your best in your role in society, you will find it difficult to be a good Buddhist. And becoming a monk will cause even more problems. Only when you fulfill the requirements of being truly human should you consider "leaving home."

Leaving the household to become
a monk or a nun is an event that takes
place within a single lifetime.
Cultivating the Path is an event
occurring over many lives and kalpas.

True Ch'an masters follow the precepts strictly, but many so-called practitioners underestimate masters who follow the precepts, preferring instead to celebrate the freedom and liberalism of the Ch'an school. The majority of them either have not yet begun to practice, or have based an insubstantial practice on stories about ancient Ch'an masters. The function of upholding precepts is not only to prevent our faith from deteriorating, but also to ensure the happiness of sentient beings.

In taking the precepts, you check
yourself with regard to actions and
speech. If your body karma and verbal
karma are relatively undefiled, then
your mind will tend to be more stable
and pure. A stable mind leads to
better practice, which in turn can lead
to samadhi. Thus the attainment of
samadhi is dependent on the practice
of the precepts.

Buddhist practitioners should place equal emphasis on the studies of *sila, samadhi,* and *prajna. Sila* and *vinaya* are the constituents and expression of Buddhadharma, whereas samadhi and prajna are the true essence of Buddhadharma. When samadhi and prajna are attained and fused into one whole, the practitioner will naturally uphold the precepts in a pure manner, just as a healthy, solid and deep-rooted tree naturally bears flourishing leaves and branches.

Precepts exist to prevent wrongdoing and to put an end to bad
retribution. When we take hold of the
precepts, we surround ourselves with
a fort, which limits us to a certain area
so that the temptations of the external
world will not manipulate us into
creating negative karma. In other
words, we hold on to precepts
because the world presents us with
more enticements than we can resist
without protection.

Wise people always hide their knowledge. Even though their understanding may be deep, they remain as "humble as the valley." On the other hand, those who know little are always afraid that others will look down on them. Because of their fear, they're always displaying their knowledge and showing off their talent. No matter how articulate and eloquent they are, however, others recognize their superficiality.

If we are to thoroughly cultivate the
path of practice, we must first use the
five precepts to help us distinguish
right from wrong. Those who can do
so develop good judgment. Those
who confuse right and wrong are
either ignorant of their behavior or are
pretending to be good while their true
intentions, in fact, lie elsewhere.
Human virtue stems from our ability
to distinguish good and evil, just as
we clearly distinguish fire and water,
and to know that, like fire and water,
good and evil each possess special
characteristics.

Cultivation practice can be separated into two stages. The first stage is when you know of the existence of a method but pay no attention to the mind. The second stage is when you are aware of the mind, without being aware of the method. The first stage occurs when you are concentrated on the method and have forgotten about your mental activities. In the latter stage, you rely neither on the method nor on internal and external environments. At this point, the only awareness is of the existence of freedom and ease.

In Mahayana meditation, you must give equal weight to both samatha and vipassana practices. In the beginning, you should cultivate samatha to collect a scattered mind and place it at one point. Afterwards, through contemplative practice, or vipassana, you give rise to wisdom in order to broaden the mind and develop insight. A practitioner has to alternate between samatha and vipassana. Liken it to climbing stairs, where you rest after each step upward. Going up the stairs is vipassana and stopping is samatha. By practicing both alternately, your skill will progress to the level where samatha and vipassana fuse into one method. This is the objective of Mahayana meditation.

The practice of Buddhadharma involves cultivating merit, samadhi, and prajna. However, if you only practice merit and samadhi and do not foster prajna, then even though you may be reborn in heavenly or dhyana realms, you will never transcend samsara. Emphasizing prajna and samadhi, but not also emphasizing merit, can lead you out of samsara to become a Hinayana arhat. Mahayana practitioners must give equal weight to merit, samadhi and prajna. This is the Bodhisattva Path.

We can define samadhi in two ways: The superficial meaning is that body and mind are unmoving, while the higher meaning is that the mind remains unperturbed in myriad situations. When there is even the slightest sensation or feeling of the existence of body and mind, then everything is an illusion.

In meditation, one approach to curing our wandering thoughts can be likened to a cat catching rats. The cat is the method of practice and the rats are the wandering thoughts. Sometimes our minds search frantically for thoughts, just like starving rats scramble to find food outside their holes. But if a cat is alert and does its job of keeping watch in front of the hole, then the rats will not dare to come out and eventually will perish from starvation.

I encourage people to penetrate their methods thoroughly. Switching methods of practice gets you nowhere. However, you can use a main method of practice and other supporting methods, or you can use preparatory methods before practicing an advanced method. Fundamentally, all methods are the same. Even though you may have great faith in the method you are currently using, you should not reject or criticize other methods of practice.

Two great obstructions to cultivating samadhi are scattered mind and drowsiness. In the early stages of practice, you will realize that your mind is either agitated and scattered or unclear and drowsy. The cultivation of vipassana cures drowsiness, while the cultivation of samatha cures scattered mind.

There are two general approaches for dealing with scattered mind: One is to gather all scattered thoughts and focus them on a single point, which is the method of practice. If this does not work, the second approach is simply to let go of your method and rest in unfabricated naturalness, detached from your thoughts, which permits the mind to settle by itself.

As for drowsiness, as soon as you feel sleepiness coming on, straighten your back. Do some deep breathing. If deep breathing alone does not work, you can couple it with hunching your shoulders and then relaxing them. You can also stare in front of you with wide-open eyes, until they well with tears. All these techniques help to clear a drowsy mind. If your mind feels lazy, contemplate the transience of life and the rare opportunity to encounter Buddhadharma.

Remember, many people only
practice diligently when they are in a
diligent mood. When they do not feel
diligent, their practice slackens. They
only see the usefulness of practice
when they are progressing. When
they feel they are regressing, they
find it hard to recognize the need to
continue diligently in their practice.

Trying to unify the mind is completely different from seeking to unify the external world. Most of the time, the external world lies outside your control. You need to alleviate the conflicts and problems of the inner world before thinking about resolving your conflicts with others.

The mind that makes no distinctions is unmoving; there are no ups and downs. If you tried to eliminate the ups and downs it would be like trying to calm the ripples on water in a pan. You want the surface to be completely still; you blow on the water to flatten it out, and end up making more ripples. Then you press the water with your hands to stop it from moving, which creates even more agitation. If you were to leave the water alone, the ripples would eventually subside and the surface would be still.

Those who are anxious cannot reach samadhi nor attain enlightenment; their worry and impatience drives them to continually compare themselves with others, which in turn generates a mind of gain and loss. You should not compare yourself with others nor with great practitioners of the past. Do not measure your past gains and losses against your present situation. Practice simply for the sake of practice and accept circumstances as they arise. Realize your mistakes and go forward; make up your mind to apply your method to your daily life. Be vigorous and hard working, but let go of your anxiety.

Those who are in a hurry to become enlightened are like caterpillars rushing out of their cocoons to become butterflies. Their haste ensures that they will either die in the process or be killed by predators.

A saying from Ch'an lore: "Suddenly casting aside the knife, the butcher immediately becomes a Buddha!" However, don't be deluded by this phrase, which does not imply that the butcher attains ultimate Buddhahood. It means only that he begins to walk on the correct path toward Buddhahood. Learning to meditate is like casting aside the butcher's knife. Just begin by adjusting your mind to accord with the Path and don't set your goals too high.

Hold on firmly to the method of cultivation. Practice is like climbing a glass mountain covered with oil. It is very slippery, with nothing to grasp and nowhere to get a foothold. Climb up and you will slide down. Climb up and you will slide down again. But you must persist. In the end, wham! You will suddenly fall down, but where will you fall? On the summit of the mountain. Why? Because there is no glass mountain.

The principle of practice is to not fear the rising of thoughts, but to fear becoming aware of them too late. Thoughts are illusory. Awareness is knowing that you have illusory thoughts.

Your brain should be like a
warehouse, an orderly storage
place. Your minds should be like a
wall, useful but unmoving.

The methods of Ch'an teach us how to go from a scattered mind to a unified mind, from unified mind to samadhi. At this level, we make use of the hua-t'ou method to shatter samadhi and enlighten our minds. At this enlightened level, samadhi and prajna are one and thoughts of good and evil are transcended.

Kung-an practice is meant to be investigated, not explained. Similarly, after enlightenment you find words and language incapable of explaining the enlightened state. Direct communication can only be made with other enlightened people at the same level, or through gestures to those with higher attainments. This is called mind-to-mind seal.

Investigating Ch'an is a method where a practitioner uses a hua-t'ou to arouse the doubt sensation. Eventually, the sensation becomes greater and turns into a great ball of doubt. Whether you are awake or asleep, sitting or walking, eating or going to the toilet, at all times the doubt is continuous, fused into one whole without a single gap. Water cannot seep in, wind cannot pass through it. This is called "pervasive practice."

Practicing a method is like riding a
horse. In the beginning you are
wholly concentrated on riding the
horse, yet it is inevitable that you will
fall often. With persistence, however,
you learn to hold your seat; and
eventually you ride so well and
naturally that you are as one with the
horse. Real riding begins when you
are unaware of the distinction
between yourself and the horse.

In your daily lives, walk single-mindedly when you walk, sleep single-mindedly when you sleep. No matter what you do, do it single-mindedly, without a second use for the mind, without external distractions, without interfering thoughts. This is self-discipline!

The basic prerequisite for Ch'an practice is to live fully in the present moment. Every word and action is a part of practice. Put your mind wholly on every moment in your life. Don't be like the headless fly that bumps into everything in its sightless flight.

Be polite to those who are good to you. Have sympathy for those who are suffering. Be respectful toward virtuous people. Extend your compassion toward those who are bad. When your mind's capacity is this large, you harmonize with purity.

For practitioners, the mind set
on the Path is primary, health is
secondary, and knowledge comes last.

Greedy people are usually unaware of their own greed. The same is true of people filled with anger, arrogance and pride. But sooner or later, practitioners will recognize that they have been greedy, angry or arrogant. At that time they should generate a sense of humility and practice repentance. If you can do this every time you recognize these feelings, these non-virtuous mental states, you will find they arise less and less frequently.

Unenlightened people must adhere
to the principles of the phenomenal
world. A practitioner should start by
relating to others peacefully, then treat
all living beings peacefully. When
facing problems, do not give in to
anger. It will only make matters more
difficult, leaving your mind vexed and
afflicted. Use a peaceful mind to avoid
anger. In this way, the problem will
naturally dissolve or transform into
something better.

Stilling the mind is like catching a feather with a fan – the old fashioned hand-held type. Every time you move the fan, the feather is likely to be blown away. It is a delicate business. You have to hold the fan quite still, just beneath the feather's downward trajectory. You can imagine how difficult, and yet how easy, this task might be!

When talking about broad topics like peace, reflect on your personal limitations. Strive primarily to achieve harmony of body and mind, and then gradually extend this harmony to your surroundings. Eventually, you will be able to merge with the numerous worlds of living beings throughout the Dharmadhatu, and with all the Buddhas in the ten directions and the three periods of time.

As a rule, practitioners should be extra-observant, extra-attentive, but under-talkative. Their hands should be quick when helping others, but cautious when spending money.

In your practice, don't pursue
extraordinary experiences. Rather,
settle your mind in the reality of
the "present moment." Only by
continuously working in the present
moment will you transform yourself
and improve. Wanting novel
experiences and breakthroughs is
like wanting to eat yet refusing to
open your mouth, or hoping for a big
salary without working for it. These
are delusions, turning the law of cause
and consequence upside down.

Those who truly know how to cultivate practice find it easier than resting, while those who do not understand cultivation find practice harder than the most difficult labor. The Buddha said that cultivation is like tuning a musical instrument: the strings must be neither too tight nor too loose.

"Great Death" in Ch'an practice
refers to the death of the deluded
mind. At the start of practice, the
mind that loves the physical body
must die, because what comes with
this mind are the five desires. They
are like five ropes tying you to
vexations, preventing you from
breaking free.

Knowing how to be a person and how to deal with others is different from the task of cultivation. As people, we should be well-rounded. If we are too direct or naive, we can harm others and also ourselves. We should be reasonable, have consideration for others, reflect before acting and consider the possible outcomes. But with cultivation, such forethought becomes unnecessary. When it is time to be compliant we are compliant. When it's time to be direct, we are direct. There is only one way to walk the Path – Straight Ahead!

The only thing to do in the course of cultivation is to keep moving forward. Like a rocket shooting into the sky, we must keep discarding sections until there is nothing more to let go of. And when there is nothing in the mind, then let go of it. Let go even of letting go.

Ch'an is a lively practice. Ch'an does not neglect the world. The Sixth Patriarch said, "Samadhi is not Ch'an." Practitioners of Ch'an lead normal lives. They do not speak of oneness or emptiness. The only difference is that their minds are free of obstructions and attachments.

Imagine that two people are coming to visit you. One lives a hundred miles away and the other a mile away. The one who lives a mile away may be the one to come late, since living so close makes him complacent. Distance is not absolute. This applies to cultivation as well. A person may generate the mind for practice late in life, but attain Buddhahood sooner than a person who started practicing early on. Those who have faith, confidence and a willingness to truly practice are closest to Buddhahood.

The true state of No Mind is the unmoving mind, which does not leave any traces. Precisely because the mind is unmoving, it spontaneously and accordingly reflects the various phenomena it encounters. Because the unmoving mind "leaves no trace," each phenomenon is clearly reflected without distortion. Practitioners who have reached the state of No Mind do not generate vexations, only wisdom.

Ultimately, Buddhadharma has nothing in particular to teach. In genuine enlightenment, there's nothing to attain. Real transcendence to the other "shore" means that there is no other "shore" to reach. When you remain attached to a goal or to the attaining of enlightenment, then that state is like the Transformation City in the *Saddharmapundharika Sutra*. The city is created for those who have completed part of a long, tiresome journey and are considering giving up the rest of the trip.

Birth and Death

Not being liberated from the transmigration of birth and death is like dreaming through an eternal night that never turns into day. Some dreams are beautiful, others are dreadful, and some are simply confusing and hazy. Among these many dreams, the good dreams are the fewest.

The reason people cherish life is because they fear death. For the individual, fear is protection against tragedy: When a common person reaches the point of not fearing for his mortality, he embarks on the path that leads to social chaos, harm to the self and others, and ultimately and ironically, to death.

Attachment to external and
internal states are causes of birth
and death. Desire for material goods
is a cause of birth and death.
Being obsessed with enlightenment
is also a cause of birth and death.

Even though sentient beings cherish life and fear death, we all must die and be born, be born and then die. Sometimes we must die when we are not willing to do so. And we have no choice over the environment in which we are born. This process of birth and death is like a flow of history without a beginning or an end, so it is called "the ocean of suffering."

Buddhism is the "great liberation pathway" out of birth and death. However, if practitioners study Buddhism, read the sutras, and practice the Dharma, but never think about liberation from birth and death, then they are like people on a treasure hunt who enter a mountain full of diamonds and jewels, but bring back only bits of earth and stones. How stupid!

The motivation for becoming a Buddhist should be related to the question of birth and death. Those in the Pure Land school should have as their goal the intention of being reborn in the Western Pure Land. Those cultivating Ch'an should strive for self-mastery, the ability to be fully liberated without leaving the transmigration of birth and death.

Death is just one step away from birth. You have already taken the step of birth, so of course the next step must be taken. Life and death are a continuous progression.

No matter how great a loss is, if you fully accept it straight on, the loss will turn out to be a gain. The great affair of birth and death works in a similar way. If you neither attach to nor fear birth and death, but boldly accept their reality, then you will become a liberated person in the midst of an ocean of suffering.

True cultivation depends on your daily diligence. Practice at all times. There is no need to worry about where you will go after death. If you give equal weight to faith and vows in your practice, you will be fearless as to where your karma will lead you after death.

It is important to set a direction in life. If you have practiced diligently all your life, you have established a direction for living. This direction becomes part of your karma. In your next life the tendency will continue; you will keep moving forward to the place where illusory thoughts disappear. You will be like a tree tied by a rope that pulls it in a certain direction, say, toward the east. Season after season, when the tree puts forth new growth, it will continue to grow in an easterly direction.

Unlike money and possessions, life is limited. Let's say we live for a hundred years. At sixteen breaths per minute we have, at most, 840,000,000 breaths in our lives. That is all. Money, on the other hand, can be earned and spent. After spending it, it can be earned again. But with every breath we take, we are left with fewer breaths.

Life is much the same as making and projecting a movie. Film moves at about ten images per second. When the movie is completed, it can be projected at the same speed that it was taken, showing the same images again. However, the movie itself is not reality. It is made of single frames of still images, and between each image is a certain time interval. Thus, the projection of events does not occur in continuous, real time. Life, too, is like this. One thought follows another in succession. If you disconnected successive thoughts, you would not see this thing called life.

If you let go of every object of
thought, you will be indistinguishable
from everything, and you will
disappear. Today someone remarked,
"I still have a self left. I have to get
rid of this self." I said, "Self is not
something you can get rid of. Self is
not inside; it is not identical to your
body or your mind. Rather, self is
precisely the object of all of your
thoughts and actions. Other than this,
there is no self."

Can your mind have no object? Usually we think of the method as something we can rely on, as a bridge to get across the river. But Ch'an is really the method of no method. There is no bridge provided, because there is no river. If you let go of your attaching mind, at that very moment you are enlightened.

Realizing that you are an ordinary
person with limited ability will help
you build a virtuous character. You
will know that there will be times and
situations in which you lack the ability
to control or change events. As you
come to recognize your shortcomings
and limitations, you will lose the urge
to commit immoral actions.

Bodhisattvas are great enlightened beings. In the midst of samsara, they are unbounded by birth and death; yet, in transcending birth and death, they do not abide in nirvana. Why? Because of their vow of compassion toward sentient beings, they manifest in birth and death.

Bodhisattvas never forsake sentient beings. They always benefit us selflessly without considering their own gain. In order to deliver sentient beings, they will continue to live in the same period of time and environment as sentient beings do.

Transmigration in this illusory world is analogous to a scene in a famous Chinese novel, *Dream of the Red Chamber,* in which a man enters the Garden of Great Contemplation and does not know how to get out. People enter this world of form, sound, smell, taste, touch, and thought, and enter as well the five desires of wealth, sex, fame, food, and sleep. Then they can't get out.

The courage that we obtain during the course of practice comes when we diligently walk in the direction of the fearless. Upon completing cultivation, we attain true fearlessness, great valor, great courage, great heroism, great power and great compassion.

There is a saying in the Ch'an tradition: "Iron shoulders carry the Path." If so, then what kind of shoulders carry the great work of the Tathagatas, who deliver sentient beings? The principle of Taoism is still worldly, while the Dharma of the Tathagatas is beyond the world. Iron shoulders are probably not enough to support the Tathagatas. Copper, silver, or even gold shoulders are also insufficient. The bulk of the Tathagatas must be lifted by Vajra shoulders.

Our bodies need clothing. Today we wear this outfit, tomorrow we wear another. Our clothes are our outer garments and our body is our inner garment. When we die, we are actually changing the body, which has no permanent, unchanging existence.

The orchid grows in dark valleys
and does not seek to be known, yet it
is sought and known. The lotus grows
in mud and does not reject bad
smells, yet is still fragrant. Cultivators
should be this modest and this
accepting of circumstances.

Where there is accumulation, there is also dispersal. Dynasties go through times of prosperity and decline. The tide rises and falls. Flowers bloom and wither. Our bodies and minds alternate constantly between existence and nothingness. If you can understand emptiness without being attached to it, and if you can face existence with diligence, then you can actively prosper without being tied to ideas of gain and loss.

From the Ch'an perspective, the terms no-birth and no-death do not mean that you are not born into a cycle of birth and death. Rather, they mean that there is no particular reality to either birth or death. These events are not things, but mere moments in a great continuity. Even though a great Buddhist sage is within the cycle of birth and death, he is liberated from it.

Human life is not easily obtained, and provides us with many opportunities. Throwing away this life doesn't mean that better opportunities are waiting for you. Murders and suicides are acts of crime and violence. To use violence to achieve your goals goes against the natural laws of karma.

As a child and teenager, I watched many refugees flee from disaster. I have been a refugee myself. In circumstances where one's life is on the line, a refugee will relinquish everything, even parents, husband or wife, and children. The minds of Ch'an practitioners should also be this willing to let go of everything. First, cast off attachments to things external to your body, like clothing, food, shelter; go further, and let go of power, status and fame. To let go of these things does not mean literally to throw them away. Rather, tell yourself that these things are only temporarily yours. They do not actually belong to you. Once you have put down these attachments, move on: cast off your body, your mind and the world.

Wandering thoughts stick to you
like ants to honey and mosquitoes to
blood. You can't get rid of them,
because after you chase them away
they will return. The best thing to do
is not pay attention to whether
wandering thoughts arise or don't
arise. Renounce even the thought of
expelling wandering thoughts. Only
by renouncing everything can you
gain anything.

People often interpret the mind of
transcendence to be a way of escaping
the world or running away from
reality. Actually, this is not so. The
departing mind is simply a mind
unattached to the world, a mind
beyond gaining or losing.

In Ch'an cultivation, you should
strive to reach a point where you can
feel at ease in any situation or
environment. Even though you may
be locked up in jail, you should still
be able to stretch and move as if
practicing *Tai-chi.* Similarly, even if
you are being cooked and boiled, you
should still be able to turn the great
Dharma wheel without obstructions.

Amitabha means limitless life and infinite light. Life refers to time and light refers to space. Being able to surpass time and be free of its limits is called "limitless life." "Infinite light" indicates the universally shining light of wisdom, the great strength that is limitless in depth, distance, and width. It pervades space and surpasses the limits of space. When birth and death are transcended, limitless life and infinite light appear.

To find your real self, you must lose
yourself. You must put aside thoughts
about your own birth and death if you
are to get anywhere. Meditators who
are full of thoughts about themselves,
thoughts about improving their
health, or of gaining limitless freedom,
will attain neither wisdom or freedom.

Transcending
Karmic
Obstructions

Before cultivating samadhi, people
with heavy or deep karmic obstacles
might not feel pain in body and mind.
But after beginning the life of
cultivation, obstructions of the body
and mind become glaringly apparent.
The best method for such people is to
perform volunteer services for the
public and to undertake arduous
physical tasks for the sangha. Instead
of seeking accomplishments, they
seek to have their karma dispelled.
After some time, their desire for fame,
benefits, and material goods grows
weak. Then, even if they do not
achieve deep samadhi, their minds
gradually become purified.

It is normal for cultivators to discover their vexations. If you do not discover vexations in the course of cultivating your practice, you are having problems. The clearer you are about the activities of your mind, the lighter the obstructions become.

When using the hua-t'ou method,
the doubt sensation that you generate
can quickly shatter your shell of
ignorance and afflicting obstructions.
This breakthrough enables you to see
your self-nature.

Hikers know that there are no passable roads in a virgin forest; however, a road will open up when you pull away the grass, thorns and wisteria. Swimmers know that there are no paths in the water, but as you swim you will create a pathway. Cultivation is similar. You only need to get on the path and walk and you will create your own path. The roads walked by the Ch'an patriarchs are theirs, not yours. You must depend on yourself to open up your own road.

In the course of practice, the more negative things you discover about yourself, the clearer you will be as to which road you should walk.

People who are free of obstructions fall into two groups. Some are the perfect practitioners, who walk on a limitless, broad, smooth path. For such people, no obstructions exist, because they find the path no matter which way they turn. The others are those who have not yet discovered their obstructions because they have not yet begun to practice. For the most part, practitioners encounter difficult situations and obstructions. But even though every barrier is hard to pass, every barrier will be passed. This is the best attitude to adopt.

Do not be afraid or get upset when vexations arise. Let vexations be vexations. As long as you are not afflicted by them, in time they will fade away.

The life of Ch'an practice is strict
and most severe. In this training,
discipline is used to change a normal
person full of faults into a great Ch'an
master of steel muscles and iron
bones, metal guts and a joyous heart,
with the face of a Buddha and the
mind of a bodhisattva. Ch'an practice
can make the timid strong; the
deceitful honest, the arrogant humble,
and the brutish gentle.

Practitioners must not only endure
suffering, but must also tolerate
temptations. The poor must bear
hardship, and the rich must bear the
danger of losing pleasure. It is difficult
to bear hardship, but it is more
difficult to bear the loss of pleasure.

Bearing hardship means accepting torments, while bearing the loss of pleasure demands the self-discipline of a higher will. By being able to endure the seemingly unendurable, we are able to observe the precepts purely.

Hardship is not necessarily bad. We need to recognize suffering and hardship for what they are and view them as opportunities to discipline ourselves. We should remember that the beautiful plum flower only blossoms in the bitter cold of winter. Accepting and working through difficulties will lead us to a better future.

There is a saying: "Good actions come with much discipline." Cultivation aside, merely accomplishing any task in this world requires the will to overcome all sorts of difficulties. On the path of cultivation – moving from selfhood to Buddhahood – obstructions will follow one after another. Sometimes obstructions actually exist. Sometimes we create them ourselves as we walk along, making it necessary for us to forge on clumsily if we are to continue.

Mara is a kind of obstructive force
that hinders our progress. All
wholesome events involving moral
principles encounter an obstructive
force, known in any form as Mara. But
the accomplishment that follows the
defeat of an obstructive force is a
worthwhile one. If we did not
encounter evil obstructions to the
Path, we would not experience
difficulties in cultivating Buddhism.
Without evil obstructions, we cannot
train our minds to stay on the Path.

Ignorance and obscurity have accumulated in us, turning our minds into thousand-year-old toilets. The greed, hatred and ignorance in them are foul. Beginning to cultivate is like opening this toilet and exposing it to the sun and wind. At the start, it is foul, but eventually the smell will naturally disperse. Do not wish for the toilet to be clean at the very beginning.

The backyard at the Ch'an Center
was full of weeds. A disciple of mine
wanted to sun the meditation cushions,
so he put them on a piece of plywood
in the yard. He forgot to put the board
away. In three months he discovered
that there was no grass growing under-
neath the board, not even roots or
seedlings, but that the area around the
board was overgrown with grass. Our
karmic obstructions can be eradicated
in a similar manner. If your method of
practice is to recite the Buddha's name,
then you only need to sincerely and
whole-heartedly recite Amitabha
Buddha's name to be born in the
Western Pure Land. After arriving
there, karmic obstructions will not have
a chance to sprout. Slowly, the strength
of karma will be completely dispelled.

Life in this universe is not in the least lonely. Looking into the past, we have as roots the ancient people who lived uncountable eons ago. Looking into the future, we are the source of people for limitless years to come. And today we are related to innumerable living beings. We are nothing, yet we are great.

Most people fear King Yama,
death, and falling into hell. It is true
that King Yama really exists, but he is
invited by the karma that we create
ourselves. Therefore, King Yama is a
condition, not a cause. If we do not
create evil causes, then there is no
way that King Yama can get hold of
us. But if we create evil karma, then
even if there were no King Yama, one
would appear anyway.

Everything we encounter is the working of cause and consequence – karma. If we always remember that cause and consequence extend to our past, present and future lives, we neither boast of good things nor blame others for unfortunate events that we encounter. When things do not go according to our wishes, we maintain a stable mind, and when everything is going successfully, we remain humble. No matter what, our relations with others will remain harmonious. Always strive to be diligent, and you will be free from worrying about the future.

As a Buddhist, you should believe in karma and causes and conditions. Accept the course of events in your life and work diligently to make things happen. Wherever you are, you should be content. Live harmoniously with others and be attentive. Only then will you truly live your life to its fullest.

When people say that the Buddhadharma is limitless, what they are actually saying is that the worldly dharmas are limited. You simply cannot talk about the limitless without speaking about the limited. This is one reason why Buddhadharma is inseparable from worldly dharmas.

In the course of practice, we must
not surrender to karmic obstruction.
We should bring forth our courage and
spirit to accept all difficulties and
suffering. By breaking through
different barriers, eventually we will
shatter this lacquer bucket and
awaken to our original face.

In cultivating the path of wisdom, anything that obstructs you from being liberated from birth and death is Mara. Strive to reach the point when your practice is strong and continuous, fused into one whole. At that point even Mara cannot touch you, let alone other petty obstructions. Until your practice reaches this stage, if you maintain an immovable faith and a detached attitude towards the different experiences you encounter, these will be enough to turn obstructions around to your benefit.

Mara is created by our minds.
Meditators should detach from
defiled impressions in their minds,
which come from greed, hatred and
ignorance. Otherwise, they will
become impediments to the Path.
When the mind is defiled, it attracts
external obstructions.

Intuition is different from prajna, or wisdom. Wisdom is the power to truly see things as they are, without perceiving the self or others or giving rise to a discriminating mind. Intuition, on the other hand, is unreliable because it is based on the self. In all circumstances, practitioners should not let the self get in the way.

Karma is not something fixed
because conditions are always
changing. Buddhist practitioners fully
accept the retribution of things done
in the past. At the same time, they
take the initiative to change their
present condition for the better. At
the least, you must strive to be good
so that your conditions will improve.
However, the cycle of karma will
never end if you don't transcend birth
and death.

Wisdom
and
Compassion

Too many schisms, too many
arguments. Religious leaders and
philosophers are forever criticizing
each other: I speak the truth, the right
view; this other view is wrong, and
let me tell you why it is wrong. True
Buddhists do not get caught up in
these trivial debates. Any path is good
if it helps to create wholesome
conduct. The difference between
these paths lies in their destination.

One day of practice, one day
of Buddhahood. One moment of
practice, one moment of Buddhahood.
One thought of practice, one thought
of Buddhahood. If successive
thoughts are in accordance with sila,
samadhi and prajna, then through
successive thoughts one is a Buddha.

It's easy for parents to know the needs of their children, but it's difficult for children to know the great pains parents go through in raising them. Likewise, great sages can understand the suffering of sentient beings, but sentient beings cannot fathom the minds of sages.

Sentient beings are interrelated in every way. We live in the same world, breathe the same air, eat and drink together, live and die together. Why, then, do we find it so difficult to experience compassion for each other, for all sentient beings?

If you haven't ever suffered, you cannot sympathize with others who are suffering. When you truly understand suffering and afflictions, you will not reject them. When you truly understand the limits of your merits, you will value and cultivate them. When you realize your ability through practice, you will learn to be humble. Practitioners, keep this in mind.

The real suffering of humans does not come from a lack of material goods, but from vexations. The practice of Buddhism alleviates our internal vexations. As we let go of vexations, we discover that the thrust of Buddhism pierces and relieves our suffering.

Offering the gift of wealth is minor giving; offering the gift of Buddha-dharma is great giving. Relieving people from calamities is minor giving; liberating people from the suffering of birth and death is great giving.

No matter whom you associate with, you should ask yourself, "How can I help and be of benefit to this person?" If you do not practice to benefit others with your virtue and knowledge, then you have only served to create debts for yourself. If you do not attain liberation, you will have to pay back those debts.

Those who cannot save themselves but try to save others are like people who cannot swim but try to save others from drowning. In the end, not only are they unable to rescue others, but they themselves drown. So whether one is practicing Mahayana or Hinayana, one's own practice should have a solid foundation.

First, strive to be a good person and hope others will also become good. Don't worry about your ability to help others attain happiness; simply give rise to an attitude that nourishes the Bodhi Mind. Then, study the Dharma not for yourself, but for all living beings who dwell in the ocean of suffering.

In the course of the bodhisattva
practice, forget about yourself and
work solely for the benefit of sentient
beings. Eventually, you will develop
true altruism: you will renounce
attachments of the self; you will forget
about saving sentient beings; you will
stop thinking about the wisdom
needed to save others. Only then can
you be called a true bodhisattva.

Wise practitioners use expedient means to help people seek the Buddha Path; these practitioners are guided by compassion. Inept practitioners misuse expedient means to guide others; they end up harming themselves and others.

In delivering sentient beings, we
must start with those closest to us.
It is our first responsibility to deliver
members of our own family.
Practitioners should reflect on
whether they have fulfilled this
responsibility.

Even the Buddha cannot deliver those who do not have an affinity with him. Regard anyone who refuses your help as a bodhisattva. If your family members are not Buddhists and they give you problems, do not find them aversive. Rather, picture yourself with regard to your family as a lotus born from fire. The more difficult things become, the more opportunities you have to practice patient endurance and loving kindness. You may never deliver your family, but they will have helped you attain Buddhahood.

If you focus only on the emotional
entanglements and burdens of having
a family, then your family becomes a
prison. But if you adopt a perspective
of compassion and patient endurance,
every family member becomes a
bodhisattva helping you along the
path to Buddhahood.

When you receive something, it is good to be aware of its source. If you take a drink of water, you should want to know if it comes from a lake or a river. If you want to drink again, you will need to know where to find this water.

If you have not noticed where something comes from, you are like a man who crosses a bridge and knocks it down behind him. He can never return or make use of it again. When you know where something comes from, you can be grateful for the source. Gratitude is a part of wisdom.

If a practitioner reaches the level where he manifests luminous wisdom and compassion toward every being he encounters, then wherever he is, sentient beings will reflect light back to him. He will recognize that all beings are Buddhas. A Buddha perceives all beings as Buddhas because a Buddha is the purest, most radiant, and most "reflective" being. On the other hand, a person who only sees others' shortcomings, who disparages others when situations do not go according to his plans, will not only not "reflect," but will instead suck the light of others! Any light that shines on such a person will disappear.

Selfless compassion and penetrating
wisdom are interdependent, like the
two wheels of a bicycle or the two
wings of a bird. Compassion unguided
by wisdom will go astray, and may
even lead to the opposite effect. Blind
love or sympathy is not true
compassion.

In shattering one bit of ignorance,
you attain one bit of Dharmakaya.
The more you break up ignorance,
the more Dharmakaya will manifest.
In the end, you attain Buddhahood.

 $\mathbf{I}$f you are humble in the presence of
those below you, you will also be
respectful to those above you. Being
humble, you will receive support from
below. Being respectful, you will win
love and care from above. But an
individual's ability and wisdom are
limited. In the absence of mutual
support and cooperation, then even if
you are determined, there will not be
any great, long-term achievements.

An old saying: "A straightforward mind is the place of practice." This refers to an ordinary, good mind. A good mind is a mind without discriminations. A non-discriminating mind is a straightforward mind. A straightforward mind is neither frank nor impulsive. Rather, it is a mind that is not twisted or distorted. Thought after thought, this mind is clear and proper. It is like a vast, smooth pathway.

A mind of compassion and wisdom
does not discriminate between races,
friends, and foes. True compassion is
vast and limitless. Wisdom reflects the
selfless nature of emptiness. Both are
like vast, empty space – inexhaustible,
without boundaries. In daily affairs,
practitioners use wisdom to solve their
own problems and compassion to help
others.

The unbiased content of the ordinary mind is natural and ever-lasting. To be natural, the mind needs to be free from anything artificially created by thought or reason, from anything shaped by experience or judgment. When these things are absent, we say that the mind is in its natural state. When the mind is natural, it is in conformity with the Path.

In Taiwanese, looking for a job is called "looking for the original path." The original path is the best path to take. You can travel many paths, but the path of the mind is the most important one. To look for the mind's path is to observe the mind's operation. At birth, activities of the mind begin. When your mind is properly directed, you are on the virtuous path that leads to the Buddha Path.

Selfless compassion is like rain. It falls on everything and does not discriminate. Still, large trees get a lot of water, while small trees, which dwell in the shade of the larger ones, get less. The rain is not selective, yet there are conditions in which it cannot be received.

In the sutras, compassion is described as sunlight. Just like the rain, sunlight is universally giving. Yet a blind person cannot see the sunshine, nor can a prisoner locked in a cellar see the light. Karmic conditions from one's own past determine whether one can receive the benediction of the Buddhas. For this reason, training is necessary. We cannot depend on compassion freely given by others. We have to do our own work.

Bodhisattvas are sometimes depicted with intense, furious appearances, which are expressions of self-mastery over killing vexations and giving life to wisdom. External vexations may manifest, but internally one should maintain a mind of wisdom. If internal thoughts of affliction arise when external afflictions appear, then one is just a common person going with the waves and following the flow.

Y ou who have not yet begun
cultivating practice or have not yet
realized the nature of emptiness are
not qualified to deny the existence
of deities. When there are Buddhas,
there are also bodhisattvas who have
not yet accomplished Buddhahood.
And when there are bodhisattvas,
there are deities. Some deities are
the external Dharma protectors of
the Buddhas and bodhisattvas. If
you deny the existence of deities,
you are denying the existence of the
Buddhas.

Avalokitesvara serves as a giant reflector, upon which thousands of people direct their thoughts. If these individuals were to direct their thoughts to different objects, they would be shining thousands of weak flashlights, scattered beams of limited power. But when people concentrate their thoughts on a single entity, they shine all of the flashlights' beams onto a single mirror, which creates a tremendous illumination. Avalokitesvara is such a mirror. Externally, this may seem similar to the practices of many other religions, but the perspective is different. Other religions say that power comes from the deity one prays to. Buddhism maintains that power comes from the individuals who pray.

The efficacy of prayer lies in the pure sincerity of the praying, which comes from one's own strength of mind and vows. One who prays often will easily have spiritual experiences.

As you would hand over your physical illness to a doctor, entrust the life of your wisdom to the Buddhas and bodhisattvas and plunge into practice. Do what should be done and can be done, and don't worry.

Religious experiences are actualized through authentic, austere practices. You must experience hardship even in the absence of hardship. Not only should you practice poverty, you must be prepared to possess absolutely nothing. After experiencing a life of hardship and poverty, you generate a great mind of sympathy towards sentient beings.

Cloudless Sky –

Enlightened View

There is nothing that is worthless and no good. The boundaries of good and bad only reflect the mind of discrimination, not the thing itself. When someone lights a roaring fire during the cold, frigid winter, we say, "This is great!" But during a hot, sweltering summer, we say, "This heat is awful!" Good and bad do not dwell in the fire, but in our feelings. True Ch'an adherents neither grasp nor reject such feelings. When they see good things, they are not joyful. When they encounter adversity, they do not become angry. Their minds are like the cloudless clear sky, unobstructed and luminous.

Wе look at a stream and we see the
water flowing. What is its purpose?
The stream has no purpose; the water
is simply flowing. Let it be so with
practice. True practice itself has no
particular purpose. If you give practice
a purpose then it is not natural practice.
When your practice has no purpose,
you are seeking nothing, you are
wanting nothing. When you want
nothing and there is nothing to want,
then what is there?

The Dharma has no fixed Dharma.
Buddhism has a long history, yet it is
always new. In the old days, it was
suitable to the conditions of the times.
In our modern age, it adapts to new
conditions.

Old friends and companions are valuable. Old things and antiques are treasures. None of us is perfect; indeed, have any of us ever known a perfect person? We may as well be practical, encourage our old, non-ideal companions, and work hard together.

Ch'an accords with science but is not limited by science. Ch'an accords with the spirit of science in that it emphasizes experience and verification, which means that you actually go through the experience of transformation.

We develop science and civilization as if we were riding a tiger. It is too dangerous to get off and we cannot make the tiger stop, so we continue riding. As science continues forward, stride by stride, the hidden dangers grow greater and greater. Eventually, we fall off our seat and the tiger turns into a bloated frog: one pin-prick will explode it in our faces.

Great scientists are often modest, spiritual people. Only second-rate scientists refuse to see the limits of science and to realize the meaning of religion; in doing so, they blindly negate religion.

A small-minded person sees everyone else as small-minded. A gentleman treats others with sincerity, and sees everyone he encounters as a gentleman. A sage believes that everyone can become a sage. The Buddha believes that everyone can become a Buddha, because the essence of all sentient beings is the same as that of the Buddhas.

Maintaining a fearless, serene attitude enables us to be youthful, joyous, and at ease in body and mind. When body and mind are at ease, we naturally refrain from committing wrongs.

Ch'an first teaches us to always observe the "direction" of our mind. If we keep the mind within the perimeter of our observations, we will not be ensnared by the external environment. A famous saying in the Chinese monasteries: "A monk for a day, strike the bell for a day." The point of this saying is that you should perform your duties well. We all have our own "bells" to strike. Clearly set forth and develop your highest potential. Your mind should be focused and directed toward the task at hand. Don't be indecisive, fickle, or capricious.

An enlightened Ch'an adept who
does not covet his experiences of
emptiness and who willingly returns
to the natural world is called "one
who has crossed over." He passes
through the illusory to enter the real,
and in doing so becomes a complete
person, one who is truly alive.

After a bird has flown from one tree to another, what trace does it leave in the air? When you stand in front of the mirror, you see your image reflected in it. But after you have gone, what is left in the mirror? Your mind should be like this; any event that occurs should leave no trace. We cannot deny that the bird has flown a certain distance, or that the mirror has reflected you. But it is precisely because the bird did not leave a trace that the other birds are free to fly over the same route, and it is precisely because the mirror does not retain your image that other people can also see their image.

Buddhadharma is not exclusively
contained in the sutras. Actually,
Buddhadharma comprises everything
in the phenomenal world. Beginners
cannot comprehend this limitless
scope, so they need the explanations
given in the sutras.

A flower seen through unimaginative eyes is a plain flower, but a flower seen through the eyes of an artist can become something extraordinary. Likewise, through the training of Ch'an practice, a flower, a leaf, even a grain of sand will seem to possess limitless vitality.

During my childhood, I lived on the southern bank of the Yangtze River. Once, my mother and I crossed to the northern bank of the Yangtze on a sailboat. Because we were going against the wind and the tide, our boat could not go in a direct path. Slowly and crookedly, it approached the opposite shore. Many times, it seemed as if we were about to get close to the shore, but with one gust of wind, the boat returned to the middle of the river. In this way, the boat drew crooked lines on the river, going forward and backward, forward and backward, until we finally reached the port on the northern bank. Similarly, in cultivating Ch'an, we must have firm confidence in the method and not worry about progress or regression, gaining or losing. Don't give up your will, keep on cultivating. Neither measure your ability nor count the days you spend practicing; just sail on.

Buddhism emphasizes self-cultivation prior to awakening. In other words, we seek liberation from self in order to develop and manifest inherent Buddha-nature. However, the compassionate vows of the Buddhas and bodhisattvas cause some to depend fully on the strength of others. Some sentient beings rely on Buddhas and bodhisattvas to save and protect them with their power. To depend completely on another's strength is superstitious and lacks wisdom. On the other hand, depending completely on your own strength is unwise as well. Self-power and other-power should be mutually supportive and helpful. By using your own strength, you motivate others' strengths; and the power of the other person's strength fortifies your own strength.

P rior to awakening, the Dharma is external to the mind and we need to seek out good teachers and receive guidance. After an authentic experience of enlightenment, the Dharma is the Mind. What naturally flows from the Mind is the method of being liberated from vexations. We no longer rely on or seek written words in the sutras because our Mind is already in accordance with what is in the sutras. However, if we still doubt certain teachings in the sutras, then we either have not had an authentic experience of enlightenment, or the experience was shallow and incomplete. In this case, we must continue to seek instructions from teachers and sutras.

All methods within the Buddhist tradition have one ultimate goal: to help you achieve wisdom. To achieve wisdom is to be enlightened. To be enlightened is to leave behind vexation and drop all goals. If you want to achieve wisdom, then start by getting rid of vexation. When vexations are eradicated, wisdom naturally manifests. When wisdom appears, vexations are vanquished. This cycle follows cause and consequence: the deeper the cultivation, the more profound the enlightenment; the more profound the wisdom, the fewer the vexations.

The greatest thing about
Buddhism is that it does not think
of itself as being great. The most
profound reality in Buddhism is that
there is no final, ultimate reality.
Perhaps some people think that the
highest truth in Buddhism is Buddha-
nature, True Suchness, which is
sometimes referred to as the True
Characteristic [of all phenomena.]
Actually, this is not the highest truth.
Ultimately, there is not even a
Buddha, let alone Buddha-nature
or True Suchness.

In Ch'an, the word "Wu" (nothingness) means not having sentimental attachments. The word "Yo" (to have) affirms that all sentient beings are endowed with unchanging Buddha-nature. Most people begin practice with an unawakened mind. Because of afflictions, we do not realize Buddha-nature; this is ignorance, and generates vexation. After attaining Buddhahood, attachments fall away and the mind-ground becomes pure and luminous. Where Buddha-nature manifests, vexations do not arise. This is Bodhi. Because of this difference, the perceptions of an ordinary person and an enlightened person are as far apart as heaven and earth. In ordinary beings, Buddha-nature is vexation; upon reaching Buddhahood, it is Bodhi.

Into enlightenment, there is
emptiness. Out of enlightenment,
there is existence. These phrases are
not easy to understand. When we
enter Wu, what are we seeking?
Nothing. Nothing can be pursued or
sought. Thus it is Wu, or "nothing" or
"there is not." But when you are
deeply enlightened, what happens?
At that time there is nothing in life
that confuses, misleads, or poses any
problem. You are as expansive as time
and space. Thus we say that entering
the realm of Wu, there is emptiness;
going deeper into wu, you return to
existence. Emptiness and existence
are not two separate things.

The lower and second-rate Dharma
shows practitioners how to walk the "live
road," whereas the highest Dharma
teaches people to walk toward a "dead
end." In Ch'an practice, to come to a
dead end means to experience the
Great Death. This means killing the
mind of dependencies, expectations,
fear, covetousness, seeking, gaining and
losing, love and aversion. This Great
Death is the moment of attaining
freedom and liberation from afflictions.
Therefore, this Great Death is really
Great Life. It is the manifestation of
enlightenment.

Buddhism is not a religion of intellect. Rather, it elevates our intellect towards wisdom. It recognizes worldly knowledge, but it emphasizes that which transcends knowledge, the wisdom attained through enlightenment. Wisdom is the ability to discern the real.

Enlightened people are still confronted with time and space, except time and space have nothing to do with them. For enlightened people, there is no such thing as coming or going. But in the midst of coming and going, they still dress and eat, and they help sentient beings according to their needs.

Those who are well known are not
necessarily great. Great monks are not
necessarily well known. Great monks
are those whose minds are beyond the
world, yet who work solely for the
salvation of sentient beings in the
world because of their compassion
and generation of the Bodhi mind.
This is true greatness.

When assessing masters, first consider their causes and conditions. In other words, their actions should be based on a foundation of emptiness; there should be no attachments in what they do. Second, consider their causes and consequences, or karma. The sense of emptiness that guides the actions of virtuous masters (causes and conditions) should accord with their karma (causes and consequences). That is to say, their actions need to be guided by a sense of responsibility. They should, at all times, be clearly aware of the consequences of their actions. Thus, there is an intimate relationship between responsibility and non-attachment.

Beginners of Ch'an practice are like
the blind and Ch'an masters are like
walking sticks. A blind person needs a
cane to walk, but has no way of
knowing which cane is best. Nevertheless, picking out the worst one is
better than picking none at all. If the
blind person refuses to walk until he's
picked the best cane, he will never
walk at all. And even if he did select
the best cane, he would be unable to
recognize it as such. Under these
circumstances, he is forced to rely on
his own intuition for guidance.

Only a great disciple is capable of distinguishing a great master. Therefore, a Ch'an adept must first have a taste of enlightenment before being qualified to visit and investigate other masters.

When an enlightened person stands before me, I will appear as an enlightened master. When facing the unenlightened, I will appear as an ordinary man. It all depends on the causes and conditions between us.

These days there are many masters who fear that their disciples will leave them. This is an unfortunate attitude. In the *Avatamsaka Sutra*, the boy Sudhana visited fifty-three good and knowing advisors, and all were joyous to teach him. If these advisors had refused to let Sudhana move on, they would not have been considered great masters.

In the past, virtuous people on the Path sought out many masters. After staying at one place for a while, they might be told that their causes and conditions were such that they would be better off studying with another master. But after they arrived at the new place, the other master would often tell them that their affinities did not match and so would send them back. Upon returning to the original master, their causes and conditions would have matured. However, if they had not followed this path and had instead remained with one master, they would not have been able to make progress.

These are the marks of virtuous masters: they have a correct view of the Dharma, their actions reveal no attachment and they have a clear sense of responsibility.

As Buddhadharma spread from
the time of Sakyamuni Buddha's
life onward, it absorbed some ideas
and beliefs from other cultures and,
in the process, became a religion.
Buddhism, however, is different
from all other religions, and its
fundamental principles are not
necessarily of a religious nature.

Sakyamuni Buddha did not teach his disciples to pray to a deity, to God, or even to the Buddha himself for help or salvation. He encouraged sentient beings to help themselves as well as others. By studying and practicing Buddhadharma, sentient beings can relieve themselves of life's vexations and eventually free themselves from the cycle of birth and death.

Ch'an Buddhism penetrates
directly to the original essence of
Buddhadharma and encourages
practitioners to rely on themselves
and solve their own problems. In fact,
Ch'an describes people who seek the
Dharma outside their own minds as
following outer-path teachings –
teachings outside the Dharma. Since
Ch'an emphasizes self-initiative, it can
do without the religious, supplicating
aspects of other Buddhist sects.

Ch'an practitioners do not deny the existence of bodhisattvas. They believe strongly in bodhisattvas, Buddhas, and patriarchs, but they do not pray to them as people would pray to a deity or God. They recognize that patriarchs and bodhisattvas are beings at different levels of practice. They revere bodhisattvas and seek to emulate them, but they do not typically ask for their help. In a humble, sober manner, Ch'an followers practice on their own, or under the guidance of a master.

If Ch'an practitioners ask the Buddha or bodhisattvas for anything, they ask for the Dharma. They seek the Dharma through the help of the Sangha and through the study of the sutras and sastras. They do not ask for power, spiritual experiences, or enlightenment. If they burn incense and prostrate to images of the Buddhas and bodhisattvas, it is not worship. It is an expression of gratitude, for without Buddhas, bodhisattvas, and the community of the Sangha, there would be no Buddha-dharma in the world. Buddhas and bodhisattvas should be taken as role models, not idols to be worshipped or guardians that protect our lives.

Glossary

A

Amitabha Buddha - Sanskrit. Literally, the Buddha of Infinite Light and Life. He is the Buddha of the Pure Land of Ultimate Bliss in the West. See Pure Land.

Avalokitesvara - Skt. (Chinese: Kuan-yin) The enlightened being of compassion.

Avatamsaka Sutra - Skt. (Ch. Hua-yen Ching) A Mahayana sutra that constitutes the basis of the teachings of the Chinese Hua-yen (Avatamsaka) school, which teaches the unobstructed interpenetration of and interdependence between principle (*li*), or ultimate reality, and phenomenon (*shih*) and between the multitude of phenomena themselves. This teaching and the Chinese Ch'an (Jp. Zen) tradition mutually influenced each other.

Arhat - Skt. "One who is worthy of venerating" and who has attained the highest achievement of the Hinayana tradition. In older Buddhist sutras, an arhat is often called "one who has no more learning," indicating that one has freed oneself from all desires and defilements and has attained nirvana (the extinction of the cyclical samsaric existence).

B

Bhiksu - Skt. A fully ordained Buddhist monk who upholds the 250 precepts of the Buddhist Sangha. See Sangha.

Bhiksuni - Skt. A fully ordained Buddhist nun who upholds the 348 precepts of the Buddhist Sangha.

Bodhi - Skt. 1) In Mahayana, bodhi is understood mainly as the realization of prajna, or perfect wisdom – seeing into one's Buddha-nature (emptiness), which transforms a vexed person into an enlightened sage. 2) The function of wisdom which helps to liberate other sentient beings. See Prajna, Buddha-nature, and Emptiness.

Bodhidharma - Skt. An enlightened Buddhist meditation master, considered by the Ch'an tradition to be the 28th Patriarch after Sakyamuni Buddha and the First Patriarch in China, who brought with him the teachings of Ch'an and Buddhist practice from India. Exact dates are uncertain, but he lived during the fifth century (CE). His life and experiences spawned numerous legends. *The Two Entries and the Four Practices* is a famous discourse attributed to Bodhidharma.

Bodhi Mind - (Skt. Bodhicitta) The mind of wisdom. A central idea in Mahayana Buddhism, its meaning differing in different contexts: 1) the altruistic mind of enlightenment which aspires to attaining Buddhahood for the sake of helping sentient beings; 2) the genuine actualization of enlightenment, awakening to the true nature of reality and the loftiness of Buddhahood; 3) selfless action. Arousing bodhi mind is the first step in establishing oneself on the Bodhisattva Path. This last meaning is extremely important yet often overlooked.

Bodhisattva - Skt. Literally, "enlightened being," the ideal model in the Mahayana tradition. A bodhisattva is a being who "upwardly" seeks Buddhahood through the cultivation of merit and wisdom (the paramitas), and "downwardly" delivers sentient beings through compassionate action based on the wisdom of emptiness. Bodhisattvas postpone their own attainment of ultimate Buddhahood until all beings are saved. See Mahayana and Paramitas.

Buddha - Skt. Literally, "awakened one," first of the Three Jewels. A Buddha is a person who has achieved Complete Enlightenment (*Anuttara-samyak-sambodhi*) and full liberation from samsara. In Ch'an literature, "seeing one's self-nature" or being enlightened to emptiness is sometimes referred to as "becoming a Buddha." In this context, becoming a Buddha refers to "getting a taste" of what the Buddha knows and sees, and not becoming a fully realized Buddha who has fulfilled the consummation of wisdom and compassion. See Three Jewels.

Buddhadharma - Skt. The Dharma, the truth and teaching taught by the Buddha. The Dharma should not be understood as a fixed set of doctrines. Thus the Buddha has said, "The Dharma has no fixed Dharma." Essentially, it is taught in response to the different dispositions of sentient beings. See Dharma, Tripitaka.

Buddha-nature - (Skt. buddhata) Synonymous with the nature of emptiness, Tathagatagarbha and True Suchness: the cornerstone of Far Eastern Buddhism. Buddhanature should be understood neither as nihilistic emptiness nor as an "object" to be experienced. To do so would limit it. Buddha-nature is the ultimate "unchangingness" of transience. Since the reality of all beings' existence is grounded in emptiness, it is possible to attain enlightenment (the realization of this truth) and attain Buddhahood. At the time of enlightenment, Buddha-nature is called bodhi. After Buddhahood it is referred to as nirvana. See Bodhi, Nirvana, Tathagatagarbha and True Suchness.

C

Causes and conditions - The concept and teaching that describes the emptiness and interconnectedness of all things (dharmas). In other words, the appearance and extinction of a dharma is due to the conglomeration of the causes and conditions of all other dharmas. Therefore, nothing arises and perishes of its own accord, but is dependent on other dharmas. As such, all dharmas are essentially without a fixed nature. All dharmas are also called "unborn" because there is no one entity that truly arises and perishes, but rather there is a continuous flow of different causes and conditions. See Dharma, Emptiness.

Ch'an - (Jp. Zen) The Chinese transliteration of the Sanskrit word, "dhyana," which refers to an Indian practice of meditative absorption. Over centuries of gradual adaptation of the doctrines and practices of Indian Buddhism to the conditions of China, the Ch'an tradition became self-conscious as a separate school during the T'ang dynasty (618-907), claiming itself to be "outside of the scriptures." During the Sung dynasty (960-1279), Ch'an was transmitted to Japan and became what is today called Zen. Ch'an emphasizes direct experience of prajna, insight into the nature of reality – emptiness. As part of the Mahayana tradition, the Ch'an school, while emphasizing meditation, embraces bodhisattva conduct as the ideal and actualization of Buddhist practice.

D

Dharma - Skt. There are two distinct meanings: 1) Dharma as Buddhadharma – the teaching of the Buddhas, the universal truth, that which Buddhists take refuge in and practice, and 2) dharmas as phenomena, things, objects and mental content. These two usages are distinguished by an upper case "D" for Dharma as teachings and a lower case "d" for dharmas as phenomena. See Buddhadharma and Three Jewels.

Dharmadhatu - Skt. Dharma-world, realm, factor, or element. The milieu of existence; the storehouse or matrix of phenomena; the all-embracing totality of things. It is sometimes associated with the ten Dharmadhatus of Buddhist cosmology, which designates the ten Dharma-worlds, or states of existence.

Dharmakaya - Skt. One of the three bodies of the Buddha according to the Mahayana view. "Dharma" here refers to the universal truth, and "kaya" means body. Together they designate the ultimate undefiled "body" or essence of the Buddha – the personification of the truth. It can also designate the realization of the nature of emptiness. It is sometimes used synonymously for Buddha-nature. See Buddha-nature and Tathagatagarbha.

Dhyana - Sk. Meditative absorption through cultivation of one-pointed concentration of mind. There are eight levels to the Buddhist system of meditative absorption, which in turn correspond to two of the three realms of samsara: the Realm of Form and the Realm of Formlessness. The first four levels of dhyana correspond to the Realm of Form. The last four levels of dhyana correspond to the Realm of Formlessness. Even though one may attain these profound levels in meditation, one is still bound by the cycle of samsara. See samadhi and samsara.

Doubt sensation - A state of mind nourished in the practice of the hua-t'ou (Jp. wato) or kung-an (Jp. koan) method in the Lin-chi Ch'an school (Jp. Rinzai Zen school). The doubt sensation does not mean suspicion or lack of faith; rather, it refers to a strong sense of wanting to know the answer to a hua-t'ou, which can only be generated when one has resolute faith in oneself, the Dharma (method of practice), and the master. Essentially, one tries to arouse this doubt, or sense of unknowing and wonder, without trying to resolve the hua-t'ou through reliance on intellect, logic, reasoning, or past experience. One must persistently question a hua-t'ou until one is totally immersed in this "questioning," until nothing is left but this doubt. Eventually, one's mind becomes completely unified and all of one's body, mind, and the world collapse into this doubt sensation. Becoming greater and greater, the sensation turns into a "great ball of doubt," which is like a locomotive racing down a railroad track. At this time, whether through the master's help or by one's own effort, one shatters this unified state of mind and directly experiences "no-mind," no-self – the nature of emptiness. See Enlightenment, Hua-t'ou and Kung-an.

E

Enlightenment - The direct, non-conceptual experience of "emptiness" of the self and dharmas. See Bodhi, Buddha, Buddha-nature and Nirvana.

Emptiness - The essential teaching of the nature of reality within Buddhism. Emptiness should not be understood in the conventional dualistic sense as something existent or non-existent. If emptiness were existent, it would be a static object, something separate from us and capable of existing as other things exist, such as trees or stones. Emptiness also should not be understood as nihilism and cannot be called non-existent because emptiness is inseparable from existence. Emptiness is the negation of the ultimate existence of anything, i.e. self or dharma (object). Because of emptiness, the multitude of phenomena can manifest. See Causes and conditions, and Buddha-nature.

F

Five Desires - Wealth, sex, fame, food, and sleep. The five desires refer also to the objects of the five senses, those of sight, sound, smell, taste, and touch.

G

Giving - (Skt. dana) One of the six practices of "perfection" (Skt. paramita) of a bodhisattva. In the Mahayana tradition, giving is one of the most important and fundamental practices. There are three kinds of giving: 1) materials; 2) Buddhadharma; and 3) the highest level, "fearlessness." The giving of fearlessness in Buddhism has a special meaning of liberating sentient beings from samsara. See Paramita and Samsara.

H

Hinayana - Skt. Literally, "lesser vehicle." A designation given by the Mahayanists for early Buddhism, the path traversed by sravakas and arhats who strive mainly for self-liberation. The term sometimes refers to the form of Buddhism practiced in Southeast Asian countries: Burma, Cambodia, Sri Lanka, Thailand, etc.

Hua-t'ou - (Jp. wato) Literally, "head or source of spoken words." The meaning refers to that place where words and language do not reach – the nature of emptiness, Buddha-nature. As a method of practice, it refers to an enigmatic phrase or word which usually comes from or relates to a kung-an. Popular hua-t'ous are: "What is Wu (nothingness)?" "My original face! What is it?" "Who is reciting the Buddha's name?" The purpose of the method is to arouse the doubt sensation and eventually become enlightened. One of the great advocators of hua-t'ou practice was Sung dynasty Ch'an Master, Ta-hui Tsung-kao (1089-1163). See Doubt sensation and Kung-an.

K

Kalpa - Skt. An old Indian way of calculating an unimaginably long period of time – eon. These are of various length. The basic kalpa is 13,965 years long. One thousand such kalpas constitute a small kalpa. Twenty small kalpas make a medium kalpa, and four medium kalpas make a great kalpa. The creation and decay of a world cycle is four great kalpas.

Karma - Skt. Literally, "action." The law of cause and consequence, to which all sentient beings and all things are subject. Karma is the ultimate explanation of human existence and the physical world. It also implies the ripening of cumulative causal results of past acts, thoughts and emotions, through causes and conditions, thus affects one's destiny. It is due to karma that sentient beings go through transmigrations within samsara. From the Buddhist viewpoint, karma should not be understood as a fixed material substance; rather, it should be understood as volition or "action." From an absolute point of view, karma does not exist in and of itself. It too is "empty" of any self nature. If karma did exist in and of itself – being permanent and fixed – liberation would be impossible. It is empty because it is constantly influenced and changed by causes and conditions. Therefore, karma is not a fixed law; that is, a particular cause does not necessarily and automatically lead to a particular consequence. However, a consequence definitely has a cause. As an analogy, consider the seed of a plant. A seed will sprout only when proper conditions (causes and conditions) are ripe. When the proper conditions of sun, rain, and temperature are absent, a seed will stay a seed. Without the cultivation of Buddhadharma, one would be unable to change one's causes and conditions and therefore be unable to stop the habitual force of karma. See Causes and conditions.

Karmic roots - The (mental) disposition of sentient beings due to their past karma. For example, people who learn quickly and can easily generate faith, who can take up the practice of the Dharma and derive beneficial results directly, are said to have "good karmic roots." This is due to their previous cultivation of and affinity for the Dharma. See Karma.

Karmic obstructions - Hindrances to one's practice or life arising specifically as a result of deeds performed in this life or in past lives. See Karma.

King Yama - Lord of the underworld.

Ksana - Skt. An indefinite period of time; a moment; an instant.

Kung-an - Ch. (Jp: koan) Literally, "public case," as in a law case. 1) In the context of the Ch'an tradition, kung-ans may be encounters, dialogues, gestures, or teachings between a master and a disciple or a Ch'an adept which usually, but not always, involve an enlightenment experience. 2) It can also be a direct expression of one's understanding of Ch'an through one's cultivation. 3) As a method, kung-an is not an issue of logic, but is a device to generate the doubt sensation. In the tenth century and onward, Ch'an masters compiled, edited and systematized these stories or "public cases" into books for Ch'an adherents to use as a device for meditative investigation. There are different facets to different kung-ans, and even within one kung-an there may be different depths of understanding. See Doubt sensation, Hua-t'ou, and Enlightenment.

M

Mahayana - Skt. Literally, "the great vehicle." A term designating the form of Buddhism which arose around the first century (CE). It is the extensive teaching of bodhisattvas who, out of compassion, put aside their own salvation and use all available means to save sentient beings. Adherents of this tradition take the Four Great Vows (I vow to deliver innumerable sentient beings; I vow to cut off endless vexations; I vow to master limitless approaches to Dharma; I vow to attain supreme Buddhahood) and the six paramitas as their main practice. See Bodhisattva and Paramitas.

Mara - Skt. 1) Lord of the sixth heaven of the desire realm. 2) The passions, delusions, obstructive stimuli, vexations and false views that obstruct sentient beings from progressing on the path to Buddhahood. 3) Buddhist sutras talk about the four mara: the mara of vexations, the mara of birth and death, the mara of five aggregates, and the celestial mara.

N

Nirvana - Skt. Total extinction of desire and ignorance, which are the causes of suffering. Nirvana may also be understood as the state of liberation through Complete Enlightenment. From the Mahayana viewpoint, after one attains Buddhahood, nirvana is the state of one's mind where the "mind of birth and death" no longer functions and the attachment to this mind no longer exists.

O

Ordinary Mind - A special expression used in Ch'an Buddhism. It is the unfettered mind of enlightenment, the mind that neither grasps nor rejects. In Chinese, the literal translation of the "ordinary mind" is actually, "the even and abiding mind," which has the meaning of an abiding mind that is even and equal. This expression was originally used by the Ch'an master Ma-tsu Tao-i (709-788).

P

Paramitas - Skt. Literally, "to the other shore." Usually translated as transcendental "perfection-practices" cultivated by bodhisattvas in order to reach "the other shore" of liberation, or Buddhahood. There are six paramitas: 1) giving (*dana-paramita*); 2) precept-keeping (*sila-paramita*); 3) patience-endurance (*ksanti-paramita*); 4) diligence (*virya-paramita*); 5) concentration (*samadhi-paramita*); 6) wisdom (*prajna-paramita*). All of the paramitas are grounded in prajna-paramita; otherwise the paramitas would be no different than worldly good deeds. The *Avatamsaka Sutra* talks of the ten paramitas that great bodhisattvas consummate. Each paramita is perfected at each of the last ten stages (*bhumis*) before Buddhahood. The first six are those mentioned above. The last four are: 7) expedient means for helping sentient beings (*upaya-paramita*); 8) vow (*pranidhana-paramita*); 9) spiritual powers (*bala-paramita*); and 10) omniscient knowledge (*jnana-paramita*).

Path - (Skt. marga). Sometimes translated as Tao. However, it is different from the Taoist usage of "Tao." In the Buddhist context, it refers to the Path towards Buddhahood, namely, the Bodhisattva Path.

Prajna - Skt. Literally, "wisdom." A central idea in Mahayana Buddhism. Prajna is the wisdom that realizes the nature of emptiness. In the Ch'an tradition, the sudden realization of prajna is called enlightenment (Jp. satori). It is the last of the six paramitas. See Bodhi.

Pure Land - (Skt. Sukhavati) 1) A notion introduced in the Mahayana sutras: an ideal place of cultivation outside of samsara. It refers to the Pure Land of Ultimate Bliss in the West created by Amitabha Buddha – The Buddha of Infinite Light and Life. The *Amitabha Sutra* states that Amitabha, while still a bodhisattva, made forty-eight vows to save sentient beings from suffering. One of these vows was to create a Pure Land of Ultimate Bliss in the West for sentient beings once he attained Buddhahood. By single-minded recitation of his name and cultivation of bodhi mind, sentient beings can be "lotus-born" into this Pure Land after death. Once born there, sentient beings can make use of this favorable condition for further practice on the Bodhisattva Path until they reach the stage of no regression. Afterward, they will return to samsara to deliver other sentient beings. 2) In other Mahayana sutras (*Vimalakirti-nirdesa Sutra* and the *Avatamsaka Sutra*), there is another conception of the Pure Land. According to these sutras, samsara is inseparable from nirvana. When the minds of sentient beings are pure, everywhere is the Pure Land.

S

Saddharmapundarika Sutra - Sk. Literally, "Sutra of the Lotus of the Wonderful Dharma." One of the earliest and most influential scriptures in the Mahayana, translated into Chinese six times between 255-601 A.D. The *Saddharmapundarika Sutra* or the *Lotus Sutra* maintains that all beings are endowed with the Buddha-nature and will eventually attain liberation or Buddhahood. The sutra describes the bodhisattva ideal, and holds that all vehicles or approaches eventually return to the Buddha vehicle.

Sakyamuni - Skt. Literally, "sage of the Sakya clan." The historical Gautama Buddha who lived in northern India during the sixth century B.C. A son of a provincial king, who renounced royal life, practiced austerities in the forest for six years and finally attained unexcelled Complete Enlightenment (*Anuttara-samyak-sambodhi*). The rest of his life was spent traveling and teaching, thereby laying the foundation of Buddhism.

Samadhi - Skt. In early Buddhism, it refers to deep states of concentration where desires are left behind. It is usually understood as an unmoving, unified state of body and mind, of the self and the external environment, or of previous thought and succeeding thought; i.e., the mind halts and stays on one thought: the existence of the self. In this state, the meditator is physically immobile. However, in the Mahayana tradition, the term "samadhi" is used in a much broader sense in which it is inseparable from wisdom, or prajna. When one is fully in accordance with prajna, one is considered to be in a state of samadhi even in the midst of activity, because one's mind is not moved by the environment and one's actions flow spontaneously out of wisdom. Thus, the Buddhas are always in a state of samadhi.

Samsara - Skt. The endless cycle of birth and death caused by ignorance, afflictions and karma. Within samsara, there are six destinies or paths; three virtuous and three evil or non-virtuous: gods, titans, humans, animals, hungry ghosts and hell beings. Out of these six destinies, humans are considered most fortunate. Only humans can both create karma and receive karma. In this sense, they are able to achieve self-liberation. See karma.

Sangha - Skt. The Buddhist community of "left home" bhiksus and bhiksunis. In the West, Sangha is used more loosely and can also refer to a community of lay practitioners. See bhiksu, bhiksuni, and the Three Jewels.

Samatha - Skt. A state of meditative stabilization, calm abiding, quiescence, tranquillity and cessation which arises after thought activity has subsided. It is one of the seven names of dhyana. In the Buddhist context, the main purpose and advantage of cultivating samatha is that through it one can develop insight (vipassana), which realizes emptiness, and thereby liberate oneself from the cyclic existence of samsara. Like samadhi, sometimes the meaning of this term in the Mahayana tradition is conjoined simultaneously with vipassana, which refers not only to meditative stabilization, but also to the simultaneity of stillness and illumination of the mind.

Sariputra - Sk. One of the ten great disciples of Sakyamuni Buddha known for his wisdom.

Sila - Sk. Moral precepts, codes of morality. One of the Three Impeccable Studies within Buddhism (sila, samadhi, and prajna). It is the foundation of Buddhist practices. There are five basic precepts for lay Buddhists: no killing, no stealing, no sexual misconduct, no lying, and no alcohol and addictive drugs. They serve as a way to protect oneself from traversing evil paths. They also help to stabilize and harmonize one's family and society.

Sravakas - Skt. Literally, "hearer, listener." Those of the Buddha's disciples who achieved liberation through hearing the Buddha's teachings.

Sudhana - Sk. Literally, "good wealth." A bodhisattva in the last chapter of the *Avatamsaka Sutra* who sojourned to fifty-three teachers seeking Complete Enlightenment. Eventually he attained the Buddha Path when meeting Samantabhadra Bodhisattva.

Sutras - Skt. Literally, "to string together." Sutras are collections of the Buddha's teaching "strung" together by the disciples of the Buddha. One of the Tripitakas, or three canons, of Buddhist teaching. See Tripitaka.

T

Tathagata - Skt. Literally, "Thus-gone One." One of the ten epithets of a Buddha.

Tathagatagarbha - Skt. It has three meanings: 1) "Storehouse of Thusness." Tathagata is "Thusness," the Buddha. Garbha mean "Storehouse," that which is "contained." So together it means "The Buddha that is contained within" [all sentient beings]. The essential nature of all sentient beings is "Thusness" and as such we all have the potential to become Buddhas. 2) It also connotes the cause, practice and fruition of practice; i.e. the consummation of Buddhahood. Since Tathagatagarbha as "Thusness" is the nature of reality, it means that Tathagatagarbha is the foundation of the possibility of practice, the doing of the practice itself, and the ultimate guarantee of its successful consummation. 3) The last meaning of Tathagatagarbha represents the ultimate fulfillment of Tathagata nature, the realization of Buddhahood with its immeasurable merits and virtues.

Three Evil Paths - Three destinies of transmigration of birth and death for sentient beings in samsara. These paths refer to being born as an animal, hungry ghost or hell being. They are considered evil or non-virtuous because sentient beings in these realms are unable to practice Buddhadharma.

Three Jewels - Buddha, Dharma, and Sangha. See individual definitions of the three.

Three periods of time - Past, present and future.

Three Refuges - "Taking or receiving the Three Jewels" signifies a procedure of declaring one's commitment to the Three Jewels; i.e. formally becoming a Buddhist.

Tripitaka - Skt. The three collections or canons of Buddhist teaching: Sutra-*pitaka*, or collections of the Buddha's teaching "strung" together by the disciples of the Buddha; Sastra-*pitaka*, or collections of treatises and discourses by Buddha's disciples and bodhisattvas and; Vinaya-*pitaka*, or collections of rules and regulations – including the sila – set by the Buddha at different occasions for the communal life of monks and nuns and laity. See Sila and Vinaya.

True Suchness - (Skt. Bhutatathata) Universal, undifferentiated, ultimate reality. "True" refers to the unchanging nature of reality; "Suchness" refers to things as they are – emptiness. Together, they mean "the unchanging reality of emptiness." In the unenlightened, its function manifests itself as the Tathagatagarbha, or Buddha-nature. After enlightenment, its function manifests itself as bodhi; and when fully brought to "perfection," i.e. Buddhahood, it is called nirvana. See the first definition of Tathagatagarbha, Bodhi, and Enlightenment.

V

Vajra - Skt. Literally, "diamond." In Buddhism, it symbolizes that which is indestructible, invincible, and imperishable. Most times it refers to emptiness, the ultimate vajra, the essence of everything existing. Emptiness is described as unborn, therefore it is indestructible. See Causes and conditions, and Emptiness.

Vexations - (Skt. klesa) Attitudes, views, emotional states, or conditions arising from attachments that cause suffering or disharmony. The five root vexations are greed, aversion, ignorance, arrogance and doubt. Sometimes "inverted views" is counted as the sixth (viewing impermanence as permanence, suffering as bliss, selflessness as self and impurity as purity).

Vinaya - Skt. One of the three canons of Tripitaka which contains the teachings of prohibitions, regulations regarding conduct and practices for Buddhist bhiksus (monks) and bhiksunis (nuns) in a Sangha. In the Mahayana Tripitaka, there are also prohibitions, regulations regarding conduct and practices for bodhisattvas.

Vipassana - Skt. A form of meditative practice to gain insight into the "three distinguishing marks of all dharmas (phenomena)"; i.e. impermanence, suffering and no-self (emptiness).

ADDITIONAL READING BY MASTER SHENG-YEN

Getting the Buddha Mind
An introduction to the profound teaching and practice of Ch'an in the context of a Ch'an retreat.

The Poetry of Enlightenment -- Poems by Ancient Ch'an Masters
Collection of poems by ancient Ch'an masters with introductions.

Faith in Mind
Translation with a lucid and powerful commentary to this important poem attributed to the seventh century Ch'an Master Seng-ts'an.

Ox Herding at Morgan's Bay
Fresh insights that explain Ch'an practice through the *Ten Ox Herding Pictures*, a well known depiction of the path to complete enlightenment.

Infinite Mirror
An in-depth commentary of *Inquiry into Matching Halves* and *The Song of Precious Mirror Samadhi*, poems by two of the founding patriarchs of the Ts'ao-tung sect of Ch'an.

The Sword of Wisdom
Translation and commentary to *The Song of Enlightenment*, a poem by the eminent eighth century Ch'an Master Yung-chia Hsuan-chueh. The poem is viewed as one of the most important works in Ch'an Buddhism.

Zen Wisdom – Knowing and Doing
Answers to questions posed by Master Sheng-yen's students.
The questions range from practical approaches toward daily
practice to philosophy and social issues.

Complete Enlightenment
Translation and commentary to one of the most influential
sutras on Chinese Buddhist movement and Ch'an. Master
Sheng-yen reveals the view, the practice, and the perfection
of complete enlightenment.